CHICK MAGNET

What Men Don't Know That Women Wish They Did.

Esmée St James

The Dating Muse
Los Gatos, CA.
Published by The Dating Muse, Los Gatos, CA

The Dating Muse
15466 Los Gatos Blvd., #109-143, Los Gatos, CA 95032

To reach out to Esmée St James for speaking, world-class coaching and advising, podcasts and media interviews, please write to **Esmee@TheDatingMuse.com**. You may use the same address for ordering bulk copies of Chick Magnet.

Connect with @EsméeStJames on **Instagram**, **Facebook**, **Twitter**, **Podcast** and **TheDatingMuse.com/Blog**/

Cover design by Erandi Ortiz Industrial Design
Author photos by Grant Atwell
Interior art by Esmée St. James

Published by The Dating Muse
15466 Los Gatos Blvd., #109-143, Los Gatos, CA 95032

For more information about the author, Esmée St. James, or for coaching, speaking engagements, podcast or a media interviews, please visit: TheDatingMuse.com

Printed in United States of America

Paperback ISBN-13: 978-1-7321357-0-3
E-Book ISBN-13: 978-1-7321357-1-0
Audio SBN-13: 978-1-7321357-5-8

Due to the ever-changing nature of the Internet, web addresses and links in this book may have changed and no longer be valid after publication of this book.

To my parents, Tania and Sandy. Thank you MaPa, for the three greatest gifts ever - my life, your love and your endless faith in me.

CONTENTS

Author's Note to Readers 7

You

1. The Importance of First Impressions 15
2. The Language of the Body 29
3. Your Eyes Say What Your Words Don't 45
4. When You Open Your Mouth 61
5. First Words 79
6. First Touch 99
7. The Sexiest Quality of All 115
8. Physical Contact 133
9. Silent Attraction Signals 147
10. Why Women Want Bad Boys 155

Her

11. Her Side 171
12. Her Goals 187
13. Little Things Add Up 201
14. Chivalry is King 217
15. Landing & Executing The First Date 231
16. Invite Her Over 241
17. Seduce Her With Cooking 253
18. Ask for the Sale 265
19. Gold Digger or Realist 281
20. The Leader 293

The Big Picture

21. Good Manners 305
22. Compliments, Anyone? 321
23. Now What? 335

Your Punch List Summary

Part 1: YOU 343
Part 2: HER 359
Part 3: THE BIG PICTURE 375

Additional Resources 381

Endnotes 382

References 386

About the Author 391

When a Woman Meets a Man Who Is Self-Confident, Speaks From the Heart and Has the Courage To Be Vulnerable, She Sees a Man Who Is Sexy.

AUTHOR'S NOTE TO READERS

"His shoes... I noticed his shoes immediately!" blurted Rita. We were at a cocktail party, and I was doing field research for this book. I had barely finished asking my attractive single friend what women look for in a man when she launched into the sad story of what could have been great but ended up a disappointment. I was all ears.

"It was our second date, and Luke was on his way over to take me for dinner at a fancy Italian place," she explained. "I was wearing a pair of Manolo Blahniks to die for and my best cocktail dress. When I opened the door, I immediately noticed he was wearing jogging shoes. What was he thinking? So I asked him to stop at his house to change shoes."

Fired up now, Rita continued about how, for their first date, Luke had shown up in workout attire. Understanding that underneath the sweats Luke was a good man, she'd given him a second chance. And now this!

Most men probably don't think the shoes they're wearing are cause for concern. To women, it speaks volumes. It's is the part where the female mind becomes a puzzle for men. Who knew that wearing comfortable sneakers to dinner could potentially turn her off?

Chick Magnet

Will women really head for the hills over your choice of footwear? Hopefully not (at least, not every time)! But here's what happens both consciously and unconsciously in a woman's mind when she sees a man heading her way:

While he's thinking of what to say to her, she's already compiling big data on him, and it's happening at lightning speed.

The type of data a woman analyzes may seem mystical to a man because rather than processing big data, his first inclination is, "Hey she's cute. I'd love to hook up with her." Most guys are just taking in the visual and thinking, "Is it worth the walk across the room and the possible rejection?"

To her, the information signals his trustworthiness as well as his confidence and overall proficiency. When a woman sees a man approaching, she instantly asks herself, "Will he hurt me?" Not only physically but also emotionally. In the blink of an eye, she draws her conclusion and reacts from there.

Women start doing big data mining with the immediately observable data. They continue until sufficient information has been gathered to process an analysis. Is he a catch? A serial killer? A good lay? A good provider? Someone to whom I can introduce my friends? The point is that you are under serious scrutiny in ways you might never have imagined and assumptions are being made using data points you may not have ever considered.

Are you looking down to check your shoes yet? Relax, attracting women isn't all about your shoes, but now you know they matter. It's more about your entire presence: what's on the outside, how you carry yourself and ultimately, what's on the inside. It's because what a woman see on the outside gives her clues about what's on the inside. It influences her decision as to whether she should process more data or move on. Her final analysis of you will hopefully include a character assessment, but if you aren't projecting the right image up front, you may never get that far. The net is details matter.

As a former fashion model and professional photographer, I've spent years both in front of and behind the lens. It's made me particularly attuned to what the "attractor factors" are between the sexes. They go more in-depth than what's on the outside — factors like confidence play a huge role in getting the girl.

How many times have you had this happen: You're at a party, looking sharp, and you spot an exceptional blonde talking with her girlfriends. You're bursting to ask her out, but you stop, waiting for just the right words or moment to magically appear when, poof! The opportunity slips between your fingers. Some other guy's already hitting on her. Argh, why?!

While looking your best is a terrific starting point if you're missing the confidence to make your move you might lose out. To get to that point your genuine, authentic self-needs to be at its best. When your self-talk, attitude, and level of self-confidence are not congruent with what you want to project, there's a disconnect. A gal may not be able to put her finger on what's missing, but she'll instinctively shy away.

You may be thinking "Um... what if she rejects the real me? Don't women go for the bad boys? Isn't it easier to use a pick-up artist line?" That may work for a nanosecond and then usually only with the wrong kind of woman.

Being inauthentic may seem easier, but you'd be lying about who you are, and she'll see through it. Lying equals cheating yourself. Being your authentic self can be challenging at first because it requires vulnerability. Know that being vulnerable at the right time is a strength because being transparent takes courage.

This book provides the key to understanding the female psyche. It reveals what she's thinking, why she's thinking it and what you can do that will make her want to be with you.

It doesn't matter if you've been out of the dating game for a while or just looking for some inspiration. Gather your courage and read on because you'll learn how to:

- Feel genuinely confident around women.
- Make it easy for women to feel romantically attracted to you.
- Be naturally irresistible to women without using phony pick-up lines.

- Stay out of the Friend Zone by walking the fine line between being safe and being exciting.
- Quickly light the spark by connecting both emotionally and physically.

Too many smart, successful men struggle when it comes to finding that missing piece of their happiness puzzle — a successful love life. They're still single because they're too busy building a career, or divorced and discouraged, or they're simply the "nice" guy who doesn't believe he can be sexy. Sound like you? You're not alone.

Let's take the frustration and guesswork out of the dating process. This book is divided into three sections to help you find love much faster:

Section 1
YOU - Develop your personal skills.

Section 2
HER - Understand things from her perspective.

Section 3
THE BIG PICTURE - Fine tune your etiquette skills in any social setting. This section is priceless because you never know who you'll meet at the next shindig.

Each section in this handbook is intended to reframe the way you think about relationships. You'll learn how to bring out the best in yourself so you can attract and pick up the right women naturally. You'll learn the cornerstones of how to start and build a relationship with someone special. The best part is that those same skills will augment your relationships with others in general.

This book is the what, why and how to stop waking up alone. And it's the core of how to become a chick magnet.

Despite all the crossed signals between the sexes, there's one common denominator we all share — the need to love and be loved. And that's what I want for you too.

Welcome to the honest place where true attraction starts.

Remember, meeting the right person, at the right time, in a genuine way can ignite your dating life and make you lucky in love for the rest of your life!

The most basic human emotional need is to be loved and to give love.

First impressions travel at the speed of light, words at the speed of sound.

Phil Sheridan

Part 1: YOU

1

THE IMPORTANCE OF FIRST IMPRESSIONS

While Ted's disorganized appearance conveyed a lack of caring and discipline, nothing was further from the truth. He was a forty-year-old single dad and to his credit, was charming and had a good, firm handshake. When I first looked into Ted's eyes, I saw a highly intelligent, inventive, courageous, genuine man. The lights were on, but it's as if the shades had been pulled down.

As I got to know Ted, it became evident that he was a man who had integrity and stable family values. He told me he wanted a family and was ready to do whatever it took to find the right woman. I said to myself, "Ok, this is going to take some work, but he's a good guy he's committed, and we're going to make it happen!"

I've developed the ability to quickly look beyond the first impression a man makes and see him for who he truly is inside. I saw that Ted had plenty to offer. Often there are hidden treasures buried deep within a man that go unnoticed, even to himself. The kicker is that even if he were self-aware, the value of polishing those unique gifts and letting them shine is either overlooked or downplayed. It might be because he's either introverted or process-oriented.

The more we keep our nose to the grindstone to be successful in our careers, the less we really "see" ourselves and the people around us. In fact, life is so hectic that most of us forget to put the brakes on and smell the coffee.

Naturally, you focus on efficiency and comfort when it comes to getting dressed, but how much attention do you give to your personal packaging? Look at it this way: You probably wouldn't approach a woman to whom you didn't feel some attraction.

Know that women will also overlook you if they don't think that you care enough to put some effort into looking presentable. And if your packaging doesn't catch her eye, you're never going to get to impress her with your witty banter, or knowledge of 17th-century garden gnomes. So if you want to get the girl, polish up your physical presence.

For starters, eliminate any obvious negatives like worn shoes and stained clothing. Focus intently on ways to project the image you seek – confident, successful, etc.

When you pay attention to how you look, people pay attention to who you are.

Here are some proven facts about first impressions:

- They're made in 6 seconds or less.
- 93% of the first impression you make stems from how you look and act, i.e., appearance, body language, and voice.
- Only 7% stems from what you say.

You know when you're having a conversation with someone you just met and you barely remember a word that was said, but you'd remember their face or other feature anywhere? Point proved! While you're talking, there's an entire unspoken conversation going on. Though they may not realize it, that's the conversation people are paying attention to – the non-verbal communication.

When a woman first meets you, she'll naturally make immediate assumptions about your intelligence, confidence, station in life, integrity, popularity and even your emotional intelligence. You're telling your story with your wardrobe, tone of voice, grooming and body language. Oh, and your words too, of course.

Once made, a first impression is almost indelible. Changing it can be done, but it will take six months and a lot of hard work. The good news is the chapters of this book contain plenty of ways to improve your odds of making an irresistible impression on women. It's as simple as understanding what a woman is looking for and then bringing your hidden qualities to the forefront. It's not about cheating or changing your core values. It's about being your best self and switching out old habits that no longer serve your goals, with ones that will draw her closer to you. Which is precisely where you want her!

Women and anyone else for that matter will naturally gravitate to those who look like they take care of themselves because it shows they care about themselves. Every man has within him a unique diamond in the rough. Sometimes all it takes is a little polish, like for instance a new online dating profile and a little confidence coaching to make that rock sparkle. Sometimes the process is more intense. Whatever your case may be, the intent is always to shine a light on your most brilliant facets.

You've probably had at least one relationship with a woman who made the mistake of trying to change you to fit her picture of Mr. Right. "Why don't you work out? You never listen to me. You're always slouching, etc." Kind of makes you wonder if you'll ever meet a gal who loves you just the way you are!

Your chances of attracting gorgeous, intelligent, compatible women will increase exponentially if you do the work on yourself up front. It shows you are self-respecting and disciplined. She's going to be introducing you to her friends, and it's important to her that you are presentable to her tribe.

Let's go back to Ted. Ted had a one-date problem. He'd lament, "Esmée, every time I ask a woman out for a second date, I get turned down. The first date always seems to go so smoothly. Last week I went on a first date with a beautiful woman in a nice place, and it went well. I walked her to her car and as we stood there saying goodbye she suddenly grabbed me by the shirt and planted a kiss on me. I figured that was a good sign. The kicker — I never heard from her again. One of my friends told me that I wouldn't know if she likes me until the third date, but I can't even get a second date. I need to know what's going on!"

The first impression he gave me clued me in as to why this was repeatedly happening to Ted. While he was brilliant, successful and worldly — all qualities most women adore — his appearance was sloppy.

He was finding women online, had a nicely-written profile and conversed well, so first dates were easy to get. Upon meeting him myself, however, I could see where these dates might say to themselves "This guy's nice, but there's something off about him. It just doesn't seem like a good fit."

When the second-date invitations fell flat, Ted would ask the ladies for feedback. It was courageous of him, and I'm sure he would have taken it well. But his dates probably couldn't put their finger on it. Or if they knew what the problem was, they wouldn't tell him for fear of hurting his feelings. By the way, women will also conclude what kind of a lover you are by how you kiss. A word of advice: Kiss 'em like you mean it. Oh, c'mon, don't look so shocked.

Let's break down the first impression Ted gave me from a woman's point of view:

Wardrobe

I'd invited him to a business club for our first session. Assuming a successful businessman like him would know that business clubs have dress codes, I didn't mention it. When I greeted him, he was wearing baggy, ripped jeans, I thought "Uh-oh, we'd better find an inconspicuous corner on the patio to talk. His t-shirt was one size too small and looked like a drugstore undershirt. Women notice these details, and they tell the story that creates the first impression you give. It turned out this was the Sunday best he wore on dates as well as important days at the office.

Facial Hair

Ted's face sported about three days' worth of ungroomed stubble. While a little bit of stubble, neatly trimmed around the edges can have great sex appeal, his wandered all the way down his neck, and stray patches appeared on his upper cheeks. The hair on the back of his neck emerged above his t-shirt line and also needed some shaving and trimming. A number of hairs sprouted from his nostrils as if they were gasping for air. The hairs growing in his ears brought to mind an old French saying: "Il a du persil aux orreilles" (he has parsley in his ears). In addition to his facial hair, his hairstyle was outgrown and needed help.

In short, Ted's grooming made it look like he'd rolled out bed late and scurried off to work not caring about his appearance. Of course, I know it was not his intention. He was a busy single dad with a demanding tech career.

I asked him if he would consider shaving, and he replied, "I thought women liked this look."

While underneath it all, Ted was a lovely, talented man, he was completely unaware that some of his wardrobe and grooming choices were reducing his chances of getting repeat dates.

One of the fantastic things about Ted was his willingness to make the necessary adjustments to himself. He was ready to align his actions with his intention — to draw in his dream woman.

Ted's vision was to find a wife he could love and cherish, someone with whom he could create a family. He had it made financially and was in excellent health, both physically and emotionally. The only thing missing was the loving relationship of which he dreamed. The fact that he knew exactly what kind of woman he was looking for and was ready to do whatever it took to attract her was immense.

That kind of tenacity and resilience made me see he was only "Three feet from gold ." (Napoleon Hill — Think and Grow Rich) Except instead of selling out, he wasn't going to stop until he got what he wanted.

Luckily for Ted, his sloppy appearance is currently the uniform adopted by many men in the tech industry so it did not reflect poorly on his career. In Ted's mind, he looks perfectly fine — he took a shower every day, brushed his teeth and got dressed. But he didn't notice the indelible stains on the front of his chinos and how ill-fitting they were, not to mention the coffee stains on his teeth.

However, to the women he was taking out on those first and final dates, his unpolished image signaled that he was missing the discipline and attention to detail that indicated he cared about himself. Interpreted by the female mind, it says "Hmmm, he's so lackadaisical I feel disrespected. Do I even care who he is or how he runs the rest of his life?"

As part of my research for this book, I interviewed Anna Akbari Ph.D., author, an expert in the sociology of style, on the subject of How to Use Style to Attract Women. I asked her "What is the one most important thing men must pay attention to with their appearance?" Her answer was no surprise to me; you guessed it... personal grooming.

It goes beyond taking a shower every morning.

A while back I dated a lovely, very successful gentleman named Sam. He was a lot of fun and always went out of his way to make sure I had a great time on our dates. Finally, the naked moment of truth came, and for the first time, his socks came off.

During that moment I was discretely looking him over, drinking him all in, top to bottom when my eyes traveled down to his now bare feet. Gaah!!! His toenails were a fright — long and scraggly, and he had callouses so thick that he could easily have walked across hot coals without shoes. Ewwwwwww.

All I could think of was, "Those things could do some serious damage once we start rolling around!" Let's say it put a damper on things because I couldn't get my mind off his feet. Luckily he got the message when I later presented him with a pair of industrial grade toenail clippers. Every woman I know feels the same about this crucial grooming detail.

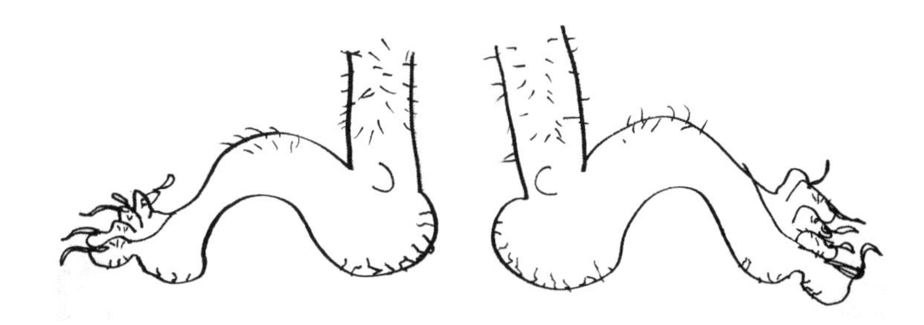

Chick Magnet

It may come as a surprise, but poor grooming is repulsive to a woman. She will not want to get into bed with you if she spots a forest growing out of your nose or a bushel of dirt under your untrimmed fingernails when you pick her up. Your odds of ever slipping those talons into her panties are zero.

When she first meets you, she does the automatic external, clothed in public scan. She calculates whether your appearance will make her look good, or whether it'll embarrass her should she choose to introduce you to her friends. But it doesn't stop there. When you get naked behind closed doors, the scanning starts all over again. It's a whole other level of data collecting.

In general, women go to great lengths to look fetching and alluring for their dates. Even if you're taking her for a hike, she'll make sure her outfit looks appealing; she shaves legs, etc. Some may take days pondering what they'll wear and even ask their girlfriends for wardrobe advice.

I'm not suggesting you call your buddies and ask "What should I wear for this date?" What I'm getting at is this — give it some serious thought. Dressing a little sharper gives you a competitive edge. If you think she's hot, chances are others do too, and you are in a competitive position. To compete effectively (for all but the ridiculously handsome) you need to invest in yourself. Make it apparent that you made an effort.

YOUR PUNCH LIST

Facial hair:

- If you choose to have a beard or mustache, it is imperative that you keep it neatly trimmed and shaped.
- Stubble can cause a painful rash on a woman's chin when engaging in passionate kisses. If she gets a rash and you like her, start shaving.
- Trim your mustache, so it doesn't reach below the top of the lip line. We ladies want to feel your soft lips, not your facial hair in our mouth when we kiss you.
- Trim nose hair and parsley ears regularly. You can find cordless trimmers at the drug store.
- The "weekend" scruff is not a good idea for a first date. Keep neatly trimmed if you do sport it.
- Short hair should be trimmed every 4 to 5 weeks. Trim sideburns and shave back of neck every week to keep your cut looking neat. Shave stray hairs on your upper cheeks.
- Keep your nails, all twenty of them neatly trimmed and filed. Save yourself a whole lot of hangnails and crusty feet repulsion. If you have calloused feet, get a pedicure. I'm serious!

- Wash your hair several times a week to keep your head smelling fresh. Rinse conditioner through in-between if your scalp is dry.

- Always style your hair. Consult your hairdresser for suggestions.

Your kisser:

- Tooth whitening is worth every penny. Spend the money.

- A pleasant smile is disarming and kissable, yours should be well maintained. Get your teeth cleaned regularly.

- If your teeth are crooked, get them straightened. Uneven or damaged teeth can spoil an otherwise sexy smile.

- Brush and floss meticulously to prevent bad breath.

Your style:

- Wardrobe — Fit and quality are critical, and believe it or not, women *want* to see the shape of your rear.

- Consult with a stylist/wardrobe expert to help develop a personal style that will make her want to undress you. Stick with your new style.

- Match the outfit to the occasion.Except for fashion sneakers, avoid running shoes at all times unless you are either going to, at, or coming from a workout, or she'll cringe thinking about what you'll wear.

I always advise my gal pals, "if you like a guy, love him as he is. Don't think that you are going to change his ways once you enter the relationship." Your mission is to make it easier for her to choose you. Find out what it's going to take and take action; make your first move to stand above the crowd.

Ted found his love only four weeks after taking action on his appearance. Now it's your turn. Be like Ted, the guy that's ready to rock 'n' roll his love life!

ADDITIONAL RESOURCES

For more tips on men's style check out my interview with author and expert in the sociology of style Anna Akbari Ph.D., "How to Use Style to Attract Women." http://thedatingmuse.com/2016/10/use-style-attract-women-video-podcast/

Fight mediocrity with every cell in your body. It's poison. Your quest for excellence is the antidote.

2

THE LANGUAGE OF THE BODY

We've all heard the expression: "When he walks through the door, the whole room lights up." It's proof that body language speaks volumes — and way faster than words. And we've all been witness to this. It's not always the most physically perfect person who commands everyone's attention, and it's not always the prettiest girls that's the sexiest. It's the one who saunters through the doorway with a confident gait, head held high and a smile playing on their lips. Usually, their wardrobe and grooming are tasteful. You can feel the charisma oozing out of every pore. Everybody's asking: "Who is that?"

Wouldn't it be nice if you could snap your fingers when entering a room and voilá, everybody instantly is drawn to you, gorgeous ladies included? What's the secret formula to making your entrance magnetic? Read on. It's simple once you see how it works.

The first impression we make is the sum of six factors. The first three — sex, race and age — we have no control over. But we can do something about the second three — body language, appearance, and voice.

In Chapter 1 we covered the importance and impact of wardrobe and grooming. They are the first attractor factors that affect whether a woman feels comfortable talking to you. At the same time, she will also unconsciously notice your body language, and it's the turning point. Unfair as it may seem, there's no escaping this fact: The body never lies.

You can, however, fake it 'till you make it — so don't give up now! It's not that complicated, but it does require some practice. I don't mean change who you are; you need to be authentic. I'm talking about making a few tweaks to become the top shelf version of yourself.

In social psychologist Amy Cuddy's highly acclaimed TED talk, "Your Body Language Shapes Who You Are," she explains that it "affects how others see us, but it may also change how we see ourselves." Cuddy shows how "power posing" — standing in a posture of confidence, even when we don't feel confident — can affect testosterone and cortisol levels in the brain, and might also have an impact on our chances for success.

I highly recommend you view this TED talk because the fallout could be a more successful love life! While an introverted person is different from a shy person, both will feel uncomfortable when presented with a room full of people they don't know. They cringe at the thought, perceiving it as a potentially threatening situation.

Cringing, or assuming a protective body posture, is the beginning of going into a fetal position. It's body language that most people aren't aware they're displaying when they feel fear. Of course, you're not going to curl up into a ball and plead "Beam me up,

Scotty!" But this posture shows up in many subtle ways that will reveal your level of self-confidence.

Take a look at the following body language examples of fear and discomfort and from where they stem. Observe yourself the next time you are approaching or talking to a woman.

Ask yourself, "Am I posturing in any of these ways?":

- Arms crossed — fear of verbal spears launching at your heart and abdomen. It is is a closed posture which discourages communication.
- Hands clasped in front of the groin or behind rear or in front of solar plexus, or hands in pockets — fear of being attacked in whatever region is being covered by hands.
- Slouching — wanting to look smaller, invisible to predators, feeling submissive and powerless.
- Protruding abdomen — the lower back arches forward and the gut is pushed out like a shield to deflect an emotional attack.
- Head down, looking at the ground — shame, and fear of judgment, ashamed of who you are and who you are not.
- Avoiding eye contact — fear of confrontation, fear of being uncovered.

- Low, meek voice — feeling like your voice or opinion isn't worthy of being heard, feeling like you're not good enough.

The extreme side of the protective posture deploys when physical danger is imminent and unavoidable. For instance, imagine you're on a desolate hiking trail in the Grand Tetons when a grizzly suddenly lurches at you, cornering you. What's the first thing you do once you finish shrieking? Exactly … you curl up into a fetal position, protecting your soft underbelly and face, and pray for divine intervention.

On the morning of my 20th birthday, a car struck me. I was barreling down a hill on my bicycle to a morning college class. By the time I remembered to look up from under my baseball cap to check the traffic light, it was too late. A large white Mercedes was about to T-bone me. Time slowed down, and the last thing I recall doing was letting go of the handlebars and curling up. My arms instinctively covered my head, and my knees drew up toward my chin. I was balancing on that skinny bike seat like some circus act until the sedan struck. When bodily harm is imminent, and there's no escaping it, we automatically curl up like a bug.

The curious thing is that when we feel caught in an emotionally threatening situation, our bodies instinctively assume a physically protective position. It's strange because we are not physically at risk. It is a trick of the mind, and we can conquer it with a dash of willpower.

When you show confidence in your body language, others will have faith in you. They'll naturally be more drawn to you because self-possession implies leadership.

Your outer world is always a reflection of your inner world. There are no exceptions; take ownership of what you project.

Like the child afraid of being scolded when his mother discovers the empty cookie jar, that same downcast gaze indicates shame and lack of self-esteem. Even though you've done nothing wrong, that scrumptious blonde you're dying to ask out may think you're dishonest, shifty or disrespectful because you're not meeting her gaze.

You'll also find that when you practice that with everyone, you're on your way to being the guy with whom everyone wants to hang. Pair that confident body language with some cool, classy wardrobe choices and boom; your foot's in the door! To find out how to kick that door open, check out Chapters 3, 4 and 5 on communication skills.

If you want her to treat you like a man in command of himself, you've got to behave like one. Take charge of how you enter the room even if it scares the pants off you.

There have been times when I've taken an escape from being on display in front of the camera and stepped out incognito. Slipping into baggy sweats, shapeless gray windbreaker, dark sunglasses and a beanie, I'd make myself invisible for an afternoon stroll in the neighborhood. During one of those disappearing acts, I decided to break my rule and popped into a photographer friend's studio. When I went up to greet him, he said, "The package is over on the counter." "Nate, it's me, Esmée!" I whispered. "Oh, I didn't recognize you. I thought you were a bike courier!"

What I also noticed was that when dressed in the invisible outfit, I did not feel like smiling at all because that disguise made me feel frumpy. As a result, no one paid me a lick of attention. Tried, tested and true, I got that "don't look at me, nothing to see here" feeling. The same thing happens to men who don't pay attention to their wardrobe or body language. They project a "nothing to see here image" and go unnoticed.

The single most important thing you can wear is a smile.

I cannot stress smiling enough. I don't mean walk around wearing a phony grin on your face. Just lift the corners of your mouth slightly in social settings or at work. Look around the room and when you catch a lady's eye, hold it for a few seconds, let that happy, confident expression gradually turn into a warm smile. Experiment with that facial expression, and you'll discover that a woman is much more apt to welcome a conversation with you because you've disarmed her with your confident, inviting smile.

On the flip side of the coin, when I step out looking stylish and wearing a smile, the response I get is quite another story. I can go to the same stores I do in my invisible mode and get compliments and offers to carry my groceries out without even asking. People ask to help me. Above all, everybody smiles at me warmly and says hello. It's a circular thing: when I dress well and look happy, people are more respectful. They want to spend time with me. As a result, I feel better about myself, and my confidence level goes up 110 percent.

So guess what I do when I'm feeling a bit down? I dress the opposite of the way I'm feeling. Instead of that frumpy, incognito disguise, I'll take the initiative to wear my Sunday best and my smile. Because you know what automatically happens when I enter a room looking like that? People gravitate towards me, and the smiles they offer back always lift my spirits. It works like a charm.

It's all about the presentation. No matter how accomplished a fellow may be in his profession, if he's walking around slouching and looking at the ground, women will assume there's either a lack of self-worth or worse, untrustworthiness. That transmits to her that he likely won't stick around to protect her from that cursed leaping lizard.

When you're confident, you don't walk around looking worried or submissive because you know that no matter what, you've got this. When you appear dauntless, everything becomes a whole lot easier.

Dare to enter the room or saunter down the street showing confidence and charisma as all great leaders do. That room or road is your arena, that is the place where women will meet you. You will not find them lurking in the corners searching for frogs to kiss.

On my bulletin board is a greeting card that I bought because I like what it says: "Present yourself as if you were a gift." To me, that is a profound statement because, in a nutshell, this is the message I want you to take in. Think of this in everything you do. It will shift your mindset from being preoccupied with what's not working for you to finding ways to make yourself a man desired by women. The instant your mindset connects with presenting yourself as a gift; the tumblers begin to click into place. Your inner diamond starts to sparkle.

Imagine you are offering someone a gift. You find a beautiful box, look for some fetching paper to wrap it up in and conjure up an elegant bow to top it off. If gift wrapping is not one of your superpowers, you make sure someone at the store makes it look spectacular.

The reason we go to such great lengths to wrap a gift beautifully with many layers is that we want to build the suspense and show that we care. "Oooohhh … I wonder what it is," the recipient will say, getting all excited. They might even give it a shake and try to guess.

You're putting a smile on that person's face because they see you care enough to search for something they'll love. Then you carefully wrap it and present it to them with warmth and a twinkle in your eye.

Now imagine that you are the gift. Imagine that you are presenting yourself to the ladies you meet. There's something extraordinary inside that you want to offer. Something she's been wanting for a long time.

Do you have any idea how exciting it is for a woman when a man offers her a gift? Half the fun for her is the excitement building within when she meets you looking and sounding so self-assured. Think of the anticipation she's feeling, especially when you look her in the eye with that inviting glint of yours. That moment is so delicious; she fully appreciates the beautiful bow and thoughtful wrapping you've used to make yourself desirable.

As she unwraps you the suspense mounts and she's savoring every second of it. The mystery is almost like good foreplay... don't get me started! Every layer that she eagerly peels back is one step closer to the precious gift that is you.

We all have something beautiful inside to offer, and when we forget to present it appealingly, other people won't see our magnificence. When you show that you know and honor what you have inside, your exterior naturally follows suit. It's the irresistible icing on the cake. Women will be excited to talk to you and discover the fantastic man you are.

But remember, it has to come from within. A guy who dresses nicely, but comes across as a pickup artist might meet that incredible woman he secretly wants, but he'll never have a relationship with her. That kind of woman will see right through his insincere facade.

Have you ever noticed how elegantly luxury jewelry stores wrap your purchase? Even if it's one of their more affordable items, they'll use the same wrapping they'd use for a $250,000 diamond engagement ring. The store does this because they know that there is always something exquisite inside, no matter the purchase price. It is precious both to the giver and to the receiver. This sentiment carries through in the attention that goes into wrapping it and the care with which the giver offers the gift.

It's not just the wrapping. It's the appreciation of how much effort goes into the giving and the receiving process. Women appreciate and want to know that you are always working on yourself and not settling for mediocrity. We're all a work in progress. You don't need to be already standing triumphantly on the pinnacle of your goals (how dull), you need only be on the path to the best possible you.

If you were to settle for your version of "good enough," there would be nothing else to improve upon, and your ambition to be more would fizzle. Perfection is impossible because invariably, the moment you think you're there, something new comes along, and now you want that. The bar keeps getting higher, and that's a good thing.

Women need to know that you are ambitious enough always to strive to be a better person, a better communicator, a better lover, etc. Why not make yourself the treasured gift that keeps on giving?

To become that vibrant, confident version of yourself that magnetically draws women in, the magic of body language has to start before you enter the room. In fact, it begins by changing your mindset before you leave your house in the morning.

With every smile you give (there's that gift thing again), you'll increase your smile score. Start keeping count of how many smiles you offer. Give them in varying degrees to everyone, including strangers. Watch their spirits lift, and yours will be too.

YOUR PUNCH LIST

To project confidence

- Smile more — it's scientifically proven that it:

- **Makes you attractive to others.** There is an automatic attraction to people who smile.

- **Improves your mood.** Try, even when it's difficult, to smile when you're feeling low. There is a good chance it will elevate the way you're feeling.

- **Is contagious.** In a positive way, others will want to be with you. You will be helping others feel good.

- **Relieves stress.** When we smile, it can help us feel better, less tired, less worn down.

- **Boosts the immune system.** Smiling can stimulate your immune response by helping you relax.

- **Lowers blood pressure.** There is evidence that smiling can decrease blood pressure.

- **Releases endorphins and serotonin.** Research has reported that smiling releases endorphins, which are natural pain relievers, along with serotonin, which makes you feel good.

How you carry yourself is equally vital in displaying confident body language. Here are some habit changing how-tos:

- Study your reflection in the mirror and observe your posture. Are you standing straight? Are you leading with the heart?
- Is your upper body leaning back from the person to whom you're talking? Align your shoulders over your hips to look more confident.
- Be conscious of how you sit at your desk. Are your back and shoulders hunched? Straighten them and keep checking in with yourself regularly until sitting and standing straight become a habit.
- Are you craning your neck forward because you need glasses? Get some cool ones. Craning puts a tremendous strain on your neck and makes you appear insecure. Bonus: studies indicate that women are attracted to men wearing stylish glasses.
- Are you fiddling with your hands when speaking with people? You may be nervous, but you don't want to advertise it. Calm your hands and separate them from one another.
- Keep your hands out of your pockets. There is nothing to hide, and it conveys disinterest.
- Avoid crossing your arms in unconscious self-defense. Keep them at your sides, odd as this may feel at first.

- Clasping your hands in front of your groin or behind your rear are signs of fear and emotional discomfort. No one is going to kick you there. Again, practice keeping your hands at your sides

Now that you know how critical body language is in conveying the sexiest quality a man can have take charge of yours. You're at the helm of your own love boat. Set your course and sail full steam ahead!

Obstacles are those frightful things you see when you take your eyes off your goal.

Henry Ford

3

YOUR EYES SAY WHAT YOUR WORDS DON'T

They say that the eyes are the window to the soul, but what does that mean? Our eyes are not just used to spot predators and pretty girls; they also expose our thoughts and emotions. It follows that women will instinctively be looking for the clues your peepers reveal.

The silent language our eyes speak is as powerful, if not more so than what our voice broadcasts about us. Regardless of what a person is saying, their eyes reveal what's going on in their hearts and minds. Yes, they even offer a glimpse beyond that into our soul.

You've noticed how movie directors always pull in for a close-up of an actor's eyes when something dramatic is happening. Acting is more than just memorizing a script. Actors use their eyes to get the point across. One of the reasons they go to such great pains to "get into character" is so their eyes can better reflect what the character is feeling inside.

Your eyes can express a feeling without even using words. Have you ever watched a foreign movie without subtitles? You don't need to be able to understand the language to get an idea of the plot. The unspoken conversation going on in the actor's eyes tells you most of what you need to know.

A desire to talk to someone and know more about them, or a desire to get away, will show in how you look at them. Our inner emotions are transmitted through our eyes by the muscles around them and in our pupils. The eyes are, after all, part of the brain.

Every move of an eye muscle is a result of something going on within us. Hence, our language has many expressions to do with the eyes:

- Wide-eyed - naive.
- Squinty-eyed – mistrustful, doubtful.
- Shifty-eyed – untrustworthy, deceitful, fear of ill motives being found out.
- Goo-goo eyed - my favorite, madly in love.
- Eyes bigger than the stomach - very hungry or greedy.
- Looking down one's nose at - disdain or air of superiority.
- Looking "over one's pince-nez" with chin down - doubt or mistrust.
- Avoiding eye contact - shame/feeling guilty or shy.

- Staring someone down - challenging them to do battle; most living beings with eyes do this.

Have you ever crossed the border and decided to save duty fees by not exactly declaring all of the goodies you're packing? Nerve-wracking, isn't it? Rightly so because for decades, border guards have been trained to study people's eyes when being asked: "Do you have anything to declare"? If your eyes look up to the left, you're usually lying about the gallons of hooch and rhino horns you've got stashed in the trunk.

If you look up to your right, it indicates you're searching your memory to answer the question correctly. Maybe you're calculating the size of the liquor bottle you bought at the duty-free, was it 750 ml or was it a liter? If you can't even look the guards in the eye, you're in trouble. Get ready to pull over and pray you're not allergic to latex. And that's just the tip of the iceberg.

Picture a person experiencing the following emotions and what their eyes might look like:

- Fear - open wide, whites showing on all four sides, pupils dilated.
- Shock - popping out of head.
- Anger - fixed and intensely focused, burning holes into the recipient.
- Joy - shiny and dancing.

- Love - soft and unfocused, eye muscles relaxed.
- Aroused - pupils dilated.

Research by Princeton University psychologist Daniel Kahneman shows that even intelligence can be measured by monitoring pupil dilation. "Scientists have used pupillometry to assess everything from sleepiness, introversion and sexual interest to race bias, schizophrenia, moral judgment, autism, and depression. And whereas they haven't been reading people's thoughts per se, they've come pretty close."

It's scary how revealing our eyes are. The good news is that you can use this information to your advantage when you are trying to figure out what's going on behind those fluttering eyelashes. Research aside, you don't need all that technical training because, as you can see, the eyes scream their message.

Now that you know what a difference it makes when you look a woman in the eyes and how you do it, I want to offer a word of caution

Don't stare! You will creep her out. Or... under the right circumstances, make her fall in love with you.

The New York Times published an article describing an experiment in which two people are made to stare into each other's eyes for four uninterrupted minutes. It's theorized that at the end of the four minutes, each

person should feel closer and more connected to the other, no matter their relationship to each other prior to the experiment.

Don't ever stare when approaching or checking women out. Note this definition of staring:

> *To confront boldly or overcome by direct action: stared down his opponents.*[1]

Chick Magnet

While I can't stress enough the importance of eye contact, when done incorrectly it can appear confrontational.

Some pickup artists use the technique of staring unblinkingly at a woman while she's not looking at him. Then when she looks up, he'll look away, leaving her wondering what's going on. Doing this will not set the arena well for you, the man with integrity, because she'll feel like prey, threatened and vulnerable. On the other end of the spectrum is not enough eye contact. Mike, a successful tech headhunter, is one of the clients who asked me, "Why don't women want a nice guy like me?" Mike is handsome, highly intelligent, interesting, introverted and a very Nice Guy. Women love him, but they were perpetually friending him.

When I met Mike for breakfast one day to get to the bottom of things, it quickly became apparent why this was happening. While conversing over croissants and lattes at a sunny outdoor cafe, I noticed the following: Mike's eyes were jumping around like a dog chasing a butterfly.

The butterfly thing was so distracting that I had a tough time following whatever story he was telling. No matter whether he was speaking or listening, his eyes were dancing all over the place. Mike's lack of eye contact created a disconnect between us. It felt like whenever I spoke, he wasn't paying attention to me. Nothing could have been further from the truth, but that's the impression he gave.

Mike had initially come to me to update his image as well as his online dating profile. Once we got the image makeover squared away, he looked oh-so dateable and was getting tons of compliments. We created a marvelous, concise dating profile that would entice women to respond to him, and we took profile photos that made all my single girlfriends coo "Mm-mm, he is yummy!"

While the results got him more first dates, compliments, and a new job, Mike was still striking out with the ladies in the long run. He acknowledged that he felt so nervous with women that his eyes would automatically enter the "dog chasing butterfly" mode. Even though Mike said that he felt perfectly comfortable with me, every time we met the same ocular dance would commence. It put the brakes on his love life.

Things changed for him the moment he began to practice better eye contact. Many men are still missing out because they don't utilize the power of eye contact. It's a cryin' shame because these men have such extraordinary qualities to offer the right woman. Women want more than just another handsome face; they want the whole package.

When your gaze is able to gently rest on a woman's eyes, there is a much greater chance for an intimate relationship to form. Good eye contact matters that much.

If a man's eyes are erratic and don't meet the lady's, she'll suspect he's either hiding something or off-the-scale nervous. It's a date deal breaker because it doesn't inspire confidence! We've all had those moments where we're so nervous we couldn't sit still. I know for some this is an extreme challenge, as it was for Mike. But if you want to catch a woman's attention, you've got to look her in the eye.

I was asked by my colleague, Dave, to help coach a group of men at one of his events on overcoming their fear of approaching women. He demonstrated an approach on yours truly for his students. The demo was so compelling when I saw the twinkle in his eye and the way he looked at me with a slight smile… wow, I was ready to give him my personal cell number!

While I barely remember what he said, I felt drawn in when he looked at me the way he did. I was so convinced he was interested that I blushed. This stuff works!

Establishing good eye contact works, and not only with women; it's useful in any situation where you want to strengthen a bond, business included. Focusing on a woman's eyes will also keep you from the fatal faux-pas of staring at other body parts, like her breasts. I know how tempting that can be, but the message you're sending her is that you're far more enraptured with her curves than what's in her heart and her mind.

Note that a very brief initial once-over glance of a woman you're interested in is key in letting her know you're romantically interested. It's a highly effective signal

Keep your eyes on the prize, not her bosom.

Just like the Homeland Security guards at the border, when we meet someone who avoids eye contact, we get the sense that there's something not quite right with them and we unconsciously make assumptions about them. Wouldn't you think they looked suspicious too?

Sometimes those assumptions are way off base. We may even surmise that the person is aloof, unapproachable or disinterested. The truth may be the exact opposite; they could be shy, introverted or have Asperger's/high functioning autism (HFA). Shy is different from introverted. Shy folks avoid making eye contact because they're self-conscious and will feel exposed. Introverted people are equally uncomfortable with getting a lot of public attention. Introverts recharge their batteries alone, at home or anywhere they can be undisturbed. Social situations make them cringe because too much socializing drains them. Extroverts, on the other hand, get their energy from being in social situations.

Asperger's is common amongst those working in technical fields that demand linear, logical thinking. My friend Tim Goldstein, founder of Technical Worker, has Asperger's. As an expert in his field, he helps tech workers better navigate the interview process with his book Geek's Guide to Interviews. As Tim puts it, "Not looking you in the eye is a common issue with Asperger's/HFA. It's not about interest, honesty, or integrity. It's about a brain that processes differently and uses different 'sensors' for communication. Summarized, what's happening is the brain resources used to look at you inhibit the ability to maintain a logical conversation. We mostly don't get any input from looking at a face. By looking away while talking we get extra processing power and no loss of the data we process."

Were you a shy teenager like me? As an adolescent, I was so introverted and reserved that I'd blush uncontrollably when a cute boy looked at me. I'd hide in a corner somewhere and think, "Oh no, don't look at me, please don't look at me." Part of me wanted to run home and read a book. Inside, however, my daydreams were exploding with a yearning so much it hurt. Later I'd kick myself for not having the courage to talk to him. It was quite the inner battle.

That's what it feels like when you're shy, and you're dying to talk to that playful brunette standing in line right next to you at the coffee shop and you just can't. You want to so badly, but your inner critic has gifted you with cement galoshes and sewn your lips shut. Easier to keep quiet and look away, or is it?

As I matured and gained confidence, I began to notice what a difference it made when I was able to hold someone's attention with my eyes during conversation. I felt more powerful and self-assured when I knew I had that connection. It was also much easier to read people because I could look into them through those two open windows on their face! Finally, I understood the saying "The eyes have it."

At first, it was challenging; especially when talking with men to whom I was attracted. With practice, I saw a vast improvement, and now I can't imagine conversing with someone without looking into their eyes. We listen with our eyes as well as our ears. We look for clues on what the other person is feeling, and from there we feel heard, adjusting the next thing we say according to those clues.

When we make eye contact, we are giving to and receiving attention from the other person. Giving attention is giving love. I don't mean romantic love but love for a fellow human being. It's also a great way to detect another's true feelings.

Did your parents make you look them in the eye when they were asking, "Who put that wad of bubble gum in your sister's hair?" Mine sure did, and it worked every time because it's awfully hard to fib under those conditions!

Mothers will take their child's face in their hands and say "Look at me" to get their attention and refocus them to get the point across. I used to do this with my little niece when she'd have crying fits. It had a calming effect and made it possible for me to talk her down.

My friend Lee's son, Joey, started speaking late. When he finally did, he stuttered so much that neither Lee nor his wife could understand him. His sister had to translate for him. Joey became so shy because of his stutter that he would hide behind Lee's leg. Lee and his wife were at their wits' end wondering how on earth Joey was going to make it through life.

When they got a speech therapist, the first thing she told them was, "Get down on one knee and be at eye level with Joey. Hold his face in your hands when you talk to him." Lo and behold, the stuttering stopped. It was powerful; it was giving love a thousandfold because of the added physical touch.

Combined with speech therapy and eye contact, Joey's confidence level grew so much that he ended up receiving a baseball scholarship and playing pro. He went on to coach baseball and taught at a college.

By now you know what a difference eye contact makes. Heck, you can even make someone fall in love with you! It's pretty powerful stuff, and I want you to be able to reap the benefits.

From personal experience, I'm familiar with the feelings of fear and vulnerability when making eye contact with someone I "had my eye on." I made myself do it. You can do this too, but you've got to do the work to learn this new skill.

Be honest: Ask yourself if you've let opportunities for love pass you by because you didn't dare catch her eye? It plays such an essential part in making more profound, heartfelt connections with women, and with anyone for that matter.

The first step is to practice holding someone's gaze. When you meet somebody new, you look at that person, shake their hand, say hello and remember their name. Don't look away.

Start doing this at work by lengthening the eye contact a second, and then another second. Do it without looking down or away, even if you're feeling nervous. Feel free to add a little smile and a nod to make it more welcoming. Practice this with everyone, not just women.

At first, a few seconds of this will feel unbearable. It's normal to feel uncomfortable. The best way to get around that is to get comfortable being uncomfortable.

It'll feel weird because you're doing something differently; you're creating new habits. Keep practicing. After a while, you'll get used to it. The eyes have muscles that move them around and what you're doing is building muscle memory. Just like playing frisbee after many years of not doing it, your body remembers how to do it.

Studies show that it takes 66 days to create new habits so do this exercise over and over for up to 66 days. Once you get the hang of that, it's time to take it to the streets. Start making eye contact with women you pass on the road. It's particularly worth doing if you feel nervous looking women in the eye.

You don't have to pick attractive women only, practice on women in general. Here's how:

- Catch their eye as you near them instead of looking away.
- Hold your gaze for 1–2 seconds.
- Let a small, pleasant smile play on your lips for another second, no need to show teeth yet. If you don't smile a tiny bit, she might think you're trying to stare her clothes off, and you'll creep her out.
- Give her a nod if you feel like it.

- If you're feeling courageous, say "hi" or "good morning" for bonus points.
- Keep walking.
- Rinse, lather, repeat with the next woman. Easy peasy lemon squeezy.

You'll find some people will quickly avert their eyes or completely ignore you. They might have their mind on something serious. Some will look at you like you're from Pluto; that's their problem. Some will smile back and maybe even say hello!

The outcome doesn't matter a rip. You are just practicing, and nobody gets hurt. You are a friendly person merely acknowledging another human being — mission accomplished.

The next challenge is to dare to do this in a more enclosed environment, such as the grocery store or some other public space. It's daring because you might run into the same woman again in another aisle … gasp.

Another excellent opportunity to practice more extended eye contact is at the store checkout counter. You know how sales clerks ask, "How are you today? Did you find everything you were looking for?" Instead of dismissing them with a "fine thanks, yep" and then burying your nose in your phone, take this opportunity to engage with them genuinely.

No doubt they're often ignored so take this moment to look them in the eye and answer "I'm excellent, thank you. How's your day going?" If they have a name tag, notice their name and use it. Do not take your eyes off them during this brief exchange and above all, smile, when you say that, pardner.

You might find that the moments you create not only make others feel great, but they boost your self-esteem and popularity.

YOUR PUNCH LIST

Mastering eye contact:

- First, look into her eyes for about five seconds. It'll feel like an eternity but the length of time you lock eyes with her matters.
- Slowly put a twinkle in your eye by lifting the corners of your mouth. Friendly is good, and it will disarm her for now.
- Give her a slight nod to acknowledge her.
- Repeat in a couple of minutes.

You may feel uncomfortable but the prom prize is this — she'll know you like her now. You're one step closer to locking lips with her.

Words mean more than what is set down on paper. It takes the human voice to infuse them with deeper meaning.

Maya Angelou

4

WHEN YOU OPEN YOUR MOUTH

Now that you've gotten a handle on your appearance, body language and managing eye contact, it's time for the moment of truth, the moment when you make contact. But first I want to talk to you about an influential part of your presence that most people aren't even aware of: your voice.

Just like the body, the voice cannot tell a lie. You can be the studliest looking guy in the room and then demolish that impression when you open your mouth. The sound of your voice will always reveal your level of confidence and your conviction in your own words. What you say can be negated by how you say it.

Imagine a young child being introduced to you by their mother. If the child isn't already hiding behind mom's leg for safety, you'll likely be met with downcast eyes and a timid voice. Sometimes that timid voice sticks around for life.

Some vocal mannerisms can drive people away. We've all attended a presentation that was ruined by the speaker's monotone voice. After three minutes it no longer matters how fascinating the topic is, you're seriously considering slipping out the back, Jack, to pull the fire alarm and shake things up little!

The *way* you say something means so much more than *what* you're actually saying.

How many different ways can you say "I love you"? I challenge you to record yourself saying "I love you" using a variety of voices: ecstatic, sad, tender, angry, indifferent. Exaggerate the feeling to amplify the difference. Ham it up! Now press replay and listen to it intently. It's a revealing exercise.

Once a woman has taken you in with her eyes, the next cue she'll be registering is the sound of your voice. Understand that the moment the vibration of your voice enters her body, millions of neurotransmitters begin firing. Should she feel afraid or friendly? Does she want to jump into your arms? That's how powerful an impression your voice can make. The tone of your voice tells a story; it tells your story.

Do others frequently ask you to repeat yourself because they can't hear you? They couldn't all be that hard of hearing. If you're introverted or shy, you may be speaking softly to avoid drawing unwelcome attention to yourself. Using a soft voice has its place for tender intimacy moments, but when used all the time it can work against you. If your usual speaking voice lacks volume, she'll think you lack self-esteem, or maybe you're hiding something.

On the opposite side of the spectrum looms the loudmouth. You can hear them bellowing from across the room, and you wish someone would jam a sock in their mouth. While the loudmouth may, in fact, be a very likable person, they drown everyone else out with their "Har-har, blablabla" backslapping howl.

A woman might conclude the loudmouth is crass and overbearing. Perhaps his volume stems from his constant need for attention and approval. Some childhood behaviors are so hard to shake off.

Let's revisit the droning bore we were snoozing to in the presentation room. What if the speaker used a bit more melody when speaking? Surely they must be passionate about their subject matter, or they wouldn't be there. Wouldn't the presentation better capture your attention if they were to go up the melody scale with their voice and then down again to better accentuate their points?

Imagine you're listening to a song that has only one note. Zzzzz-zzzz. See what I mean? Great if you want to put others to sleep. Women are much more fun when they're fully awake. If you notice her eyes glazing over, consider keeping her enchanted with more melody in your voice. Think of yourself as a snake charmer hypnotizing the undulating cobra.

As my friend, mentor and celebrity voice coach Roger Love explains, it takes a delicate balance to be able to master speaking confidently with the right pitch, pace, volume, tone, and melody. It's a skill well worth developing because it can make all the difference in capturing and keeping a woman's attention.

A strong, confident voice tells women, and men as well that you're in charge of you. And that's a seductive quality to a woman. It expresses your inner assurance in what you're saying and also your belief in yourself. It goes further because this voice, the one that speaks success, is flat-out sexy and far outweighs handsome looks.

Have you noticed the best leaders and actors always have unforgettable voices that people readily trust and follow? Think Winston Churchill, Sir Richard Attenborough, James Earl Jones. We are more apt to believe and have confidence in a person when their voice has depth, variety, and character.

When Don, a bright engineer in his 50s, came to me for an image makeover, he'd been neither married nor had a long-term relationship. In his mind, a new wardrobe and a revamped online dating profile would do the trick to attract love.

Well, those were a great start because he presented on the nerdier side. His clothes made him appear older than he was. His new look worked wonders in garnering compliments from women and everyone else for that matter. And he was attracting much more exciting nibbles with his new dating profile.

But something was missing. Don still was getting Friend Zoned by the women he met. He had such a charming and vulnerable quality about him, and yet his dating prospects were slipping through his fingers. I knew this man's potential as a loyal, trustworthy, loving partner for some lucky gal, and I wanted that for him as much as he did. I suggested we take things a step further.

What I noticed with Don was that every time he told a story, his voice would speed up so much that I couldn't make out what he was saying. His regular speaking voice was fast already, but when he got excited about something, the words morphed into a rapid-fire mumble. I was struggling to make out what might otherwise have been a great story. It was a mystery how he kept from losing consciousness due to lack of oxygen, as he barely paused to draw a breath. I can see why a woman might give up on giving him a chance. He was tough to follow.

In tandem with his speech pattern, Don's gesticulations would grow frantic, and eye contact disappeared while he was in the midst of storytelling. It was as if he went into his own little world. Hand gestures are a beautiful thing when appropriately used to accentuate a point. However, when gestures get out of hand, they become a distraction.

As Don spoke, his eyes followed his hands, and I struggled to keep track. When I suggested to him that he work on his delivery, he was quite surprised but eager to know more. He was completely unaware that the way he was speaking was disengaging others.

I asked Don why he felt he was speeding up, avoiding eye contact and flailing his arms about when speaking to women. My instinct told me it was more than just the excitement of storytelling. It turned out that as a child, both his parents had been overbearing and he seldom got the chance to speak up for himself. As a result, he started to create a diversion with his arms and accelerate his speech to keep the attention of his audience before being cut off.

Once I coached him to speak more slowly and enunciate more clearly, to rein in the gestures and maintain eye contact, everything shifted. Suddenly not only did women begin to connect with his story but so did he — and on a much deeper, more emotional level. Lesson #1 on how to be both vulnerable and masculine at the same time — done!

Don't we all have some survival habits from the past to help us get the attention we need? I sure did. It's human nature to do whatever it takes to get that attention, especially from those that matter to us most, our family and friends. But there's more than one way to get that; some habits are meant to be broken.

As a teen, I remember sitting at the dinner table listening to my dad. He was a wonderful, witty man and would tell fascinating, lengthy tales about the past. The only thing was that when one of my siblings or I dared to chime in, he'd hold his breath and shoot us a warning glance. Then he'd cut us off and continue with his discourse. Alternately he'd stop in mid-sentence and with an exasperated tone say "May I speak now?" He held court at dinner, and we learned to either keep quiet or talk fast. My mama and I would exchange mirthful glances that contained entire silent conversations. I'm still learning to slow down!

"The human voice: It's the instrument we all play. It's the most powerful sound in the world, probably. It's the only one that can start a war or say 'I love you.' And yet many people have the

experience that when they speak, people don't
listen to them."

—Julian Treasure

Getting back to Don and his staccato speech pattern, his voice also had a nasal sound, as if squeezed out of his head against its will. It couldn't have been more different from Stephen's voice. One evening at a social gathering at my fitness club, I was making a beeline for the Sangria bar when suddenly something forced me to take a detour. It was the sound of a fantastic voice. As if I were being drawn in by some invisible magnet, I followed my ears to find out who owned those mesmerizing vocal chords. There was something beautiful about the way he sounded, and I wanted to know more.

Stephen had a rich voice that made me want to meet him and not just once. Unlike Don's nasal tone, Stephen's voice came from his chest rather than his nose. We struck up a conversation, and his low, comforting pitch had a resonance that made me want to stand closer to him. I could feel the vibration of his voice entering my body.

I felt I could confide in him; his voice was that reassuring. Of course, it was more than just the sound coming out of his mouth that made me feel like I could open up to him. It was as if he was listening to me with his eyes, which to me, meant that he was paying attention to what I was saying. His body language was calm and relaxed, arms at his sides, good posture, hand gestures in sync with the words, his gaze steady as she goes into my eyes.

This encounter was so entrancing it reminded me of my papa reading me bedtime stories as a four-year-old in the Netherlands. It was the one thing that made me think bedtime wasn't all bad. We lived in a skinny row house in the suburbs of Rotterdam. My bedroom faced the street, and I loved the warm afternoon summer sun that bathed my floor. Around eight o'clock every evening I'd crawl under the covers, scoot over and wait for Papa to hop in and read me exciting fairy tales from the vast Brothers Grimm book we had. It had a forest with gnomes dancing on the cover. I can still picture it.

Voices can be like magic elixirs. Or they can be like nerve agents.

What made each story magically come to life was the sound of Papa's voice. When he read to me in that confident, animated voice, I was in heaven. It made me feel like he was all there, just for me and that no one else existed. We were in our own reality. I'd trade almost anything to have one of those moments back.

He'd speak slowly, steadily and precisely with just the right volume, making sure I understood every word. Each of the characters— witches, wolves, fairies and small children came to life with the different voices he gave them. It was delightfully entertaining. I was spellbound.

The result of all this effort to entertain me, soothe me and relax me was that I felt incredibly protected and loved. For those bedtime story sessions, my papa was all mine. Nothing could separate us; we were safe.

I'm not suggesting you whip out a book of fairy tales when you talk to women and especially not that you treat them like little girls — unless she's into that, in which case, put this book down and read the one about the wolf in sheep's clothing!

What I'm getting at is that there is much to be gained from learning to speak in an engaging, clear and confident manner. It will make a huge difference in not just how women, but people in general, respond to you.

Women want to know that you're strong enough and loud enough to make your position heard.

Mumbling muzzles you — it keeps you from getting and holding her attention. It's a nuisance to have to ask a person to repeat what they just said continually. She'll soon tire of it and move on if you're mumbling to your feet when you address her.

Her perception will be that you either:

A. Don't care enough to ensure she understands you.

B. Don't think you've got something worth hearing.

I know quite the opposite is true. You're in good company — many men feel nervous when approaching beautiful, sexy women. Women get nervous too, and it's to your advantage to take the lead in making her feel safe and comfortable.

By working on your pitch, pace, tone, volume, and melody you will better be able to communicate to her that you have:

- Personal power
- Strength and confidence
- Authority
- Charisma
- Tenderness and compassion
- An engaging personality

It may seem like a tall order, all this work merely to make your voice sound good. Keep your eyes on the prize. It's worth every bead of sweat. Remember, what you say is just information, how you say it makes it interesting. The objective is to have a memorable voice, in a good way. You know how you'll remember the words to a good song? It's because putting the words to music makes it stick in your mind. When you make your voice more engaging, you will linger longer in her memory.

You could be telling a gal that she's about to step on a rattlesnake, but if you sound like you're talking under your breath, she's a goner. What you want to do is take her breath away with your voice.

To sound strong, you've got to be able to fill your lungs with air so you can have more volume. When a man carries himself with a slouch, it compressed the very organs — his lungs and diaphragm — he needs to be able to speak with a full, rich voice.

Right between the lungs and diaphragm lies the solar plexus, the crossroads of fear. It's where we experience our gut feelings. We'll hold our breath when feeling nervous, almost as if we're anticipating a punch to the gut. Our body is deciding whether to put 'em up or make a run for it.

Sitting at a desk for hours will also reduce the blood flow to the brain and makes it even harder to sound self-assured. Get into the habit of getting up from your desk every fifty minutes to walk, stretch, breathe deeply, do air squats — anything to get the blood and oxygen coursing through your veins.

Practice good posture at all times; catch yourself in the mirror to check. Breathe deeply, stand proud, shoulder blades pulled together and down, spine straight (a natural curve is fine), belly tucked in, head held high. It's so much easier to look and sound confident and intelligent when oxygen-rich blood flows to our brains unimpeded.

Before you talk to a woman, take three deep breaths. Fill your lungs right down to your diaphragm, in fact right down to your cojones because it's from there that's where your voice needs to come. Then gently blow out the air. Take longer to exhale than to inhale.

This technique will relax you and help your brain function better. Your voice will automatically come out sounding richer and stronger. Not like it's the last gasp of air emitting from a nearly deflated balloon. Make sure she doesn't spy you doing this.

The three deep breaths trick is what my friend and mentor Lt. Cl. Special Ops Green Beret Ret. David Scott Mann would do to avoid sounding panicked whenever the merde hit the fan during battle in Afghanistan. Take it from an expert; no one follows the guy who appears frantic with fear.

This breathing exercise also enables you to slow your speech down, so you're more intelligible, a leader in control of himself. A voice that's not clear and audible will give the impression that you don't have what it takes to speak up for yourself and potentially for her. That's where speaking from the cojones comes in handy.

Adjust your volume for the situation. There's no need to shout like an obnoxious tourist unless the ambient noise calls for it, but if your voice is too soft, she'll think "Is he just timid or is he paranoid that everybody's listening to him?" Who cares if others hear you? Unless you're being indiscrete or perhaps purring sweet naughties into her ear, speak up and be heard!

The most effective way to check how you sound is to (gasp) record a brief video of yourself speaking. You'll also be able to check for eye contact and body language at the same time. Go ahead and do this with your smartphone. Set it up, go into video selfie mode, and press the red button. It's more effective when you mount your phone on a tripod, so you can relax and use both hands when speaking.

The best way to improve your delivery is to practice it. All you need is the following:

- A smartphone
- A tripod with smartphone mount (available online at very reasonable prices). A flexible Gorilla tripod will do if you want to set it up on a shelf.

Now do this:

Chick Magnet

- Set up your phone at eye level in a spot where there's some light.
- Pick a two-minute story about something you love; any will do for now because this is about how you say what you say.
- Tell the story standing up so you can fill your lungs. Speak clearly, with intent

Unless you love being on camera, this will feel ridiculously silly and uncomfortable. So what, you've got to start somewhere.

Now recite your story using the most extreme, then least extreme and lastly the middle range of each of the vocal qualities below.

Do them one at a time like this:

- **Pitch** - Pinch your nose and use a shrill, irritating nasal voice, then let the sound come from way down in your chest like a baritone opera singer.
- **Pace** - talk like you're on fire, then in sloooow mooooootion.
- **Tone** - say it with sarcasm, then with tenderness, invest some emotion into it.

- **Volume** - be obnoxiously loud, then mumble softly at your feet as if you were on your last breath.
- **Melody** - use too much variety, sing it, then go totally monotone, trailing off at the end.

Get out of your ego, discard the self-conscious thoughts, they won't serve you in being a better man. They won't serve you anywhere for that matter.

YOUR PUNCH LIST

Once you finish chuckling at your antics, review your recordings and observe yourself. Do an honest self-assessment. You'll start to notice where you sound and looks more confident, more engaging.

- Ask yourself, "Where can I improve? Which delivery is most charismatic? Would I want to hang out with me?"
- Practice it a thousand times if you have to. It works.
- Watch yourself after each time and note where there is room for improvement; you want to capture her attention and admiration with your voice and overall delivery.
- Work at it. Each time it'll be better, I promise.

Bonus: Now pick an interesting anecdote to work on, you'll have it down pat for impressing that cutie you just struck up a conversation with.

Trust me; you will find this exercise very useful. Next, reach your right hand high above your head and over to your back and give yourself a hearty pat on the back. You deserve it, and you've just done what most guys never will. You've taken a giant step toward a more engaging, sexier you.

ADDITIONAL RESOURCES

For more info on approaching women check out this video: **How to Approach a Woman. https://thedatingmuse.mykajabi.com/blog/tips-on-how-to-approach-women**

Fear is the path to darkness... fear leads to anger... anger leads to hate... hate leads to suffering.

Yoda

5

FIRST WORDS

Oh man, there she is, walking down the street towards you — the face of an angel, long, slim legs, hair shining in the sun, the breeze gently making her summer dress cling to her curves. She sashays along the sidewalk as if her feet barely touch the ground. You can't take your eyes off of her.

You have just one chance to connect with her. As she draws nearer, you feel your pulse quicken. It's now or never. But, gulp — what do you say?

First, know what not to say. We already know that words only make up 7 percent of the first impression we make on others, while our tone of voice weighs in at 38 percent. Using the wrong words, however, can still make that 7 percent aim down and shoot you right in the foot.

For lack of better coaching, many men will look to Pick-Up Artists (PUA) for clever one-liners they claim will make her drop her panties as if they were infested with fire ants. One word — don't!

A PUA line will do three things:

1. Make you look like a desperate hound.
2. Turn amazing women away.
3. Attract women with no confidence.

Obviously, this is neither who you are nor what you want, or else you wouldn't still be with me in this book.

Most successful, confident women can detect a pick-up line as quickly as they can a cheap cologne. They will steer clear of you as quickly as possible. If your first words objectify her, she will object. To a gal with class, a pick-up line is creepy and reeks of, you guessed it, cheap cologne.

Pick-up lines are generally derogatory remarks used to make a woman doubt herself, on the premise that it will make her want your approval. Approaching women this way can get you sex, but you'll end up with someone who is used to being emotionally or physically abused and has low self-esteem. She might be a nice person, and hopefully, she is doing everything she can to get through her pain. But she is not ready for someone like you.

It's not uncommon for both sexes to have emotional scars from painful past experiences. If you are one of those people, I urge you to seek professional counseling. You'll find out why in the next chapter. If you want to attract an emotionally secure, confident woman with good communication skills, read on.

Of course, you'd love to see that sashaying sidewalk beauty naked, and you want to convey your interest. However, if the first words you utter lack finesse, she'll walk on by. So how do you make that amazing woman stop and talk with you?

You already have the skinny on how to look and sound confident. It's is a significant head start on many other men. You know to smile at her and make eye contact as she's nearing you. You're well-put-together at all times even if you're only going to the grocery store. You're 93 percent there!

Use the Un-Pick-Up Line.

All that's left is for you use the Un-Pick-Up Line. Say something disarmingly innocent like this:

"Hi, you look like you have great taste. Would you mind helping me out with something, please? I'm looking for a gold bracelet for my little sister's birthday. What jeweler would you recommend? She's turning eighteen, and I want her to have a keepsake from me. Oh, my name's ________."

Be sure to use that low, secure masculine voice that comes from deep in your abdomen. It'll make her feel reassured. Remember that when you feel shy or nervous, your voice will have a higher, strained pitch like reluctant toothpaste squeezed out of your nose. It's is because of nervous tension in the throat muscles that work the vocal chords. You'll sound less manly as if you were afraid to upset her with your approach. It'll, in turn, cause her to feel nervous and want to move away from you. The pitch of your voice is entirely within your control. To master this lower voice, practice speaking in a lower voice whenever you feel nervous. There are plenty of opportunities; how about your next business presentation or when asking for a raise?

The Hi-Bye Technique.

IIf she engages in the conversation and her body language tells you she's open to more, it's time to take it a step further. For instance, if she's not in a screaming hurry, you might offer to walk a bit with her or ask her to pop into a coffee shop with you. Here's the magic part: Tell her you only have a few minutes, so she doesn't feel pressured. It'll also gives you both a graceful out, should she not be interested.

As you bid her goodbye, say something like, "Wow, you've been so helpful. I'd love to take you for a glass of wine." Now pull out your phone and ask for her number so you can reach her. Then text her right there so you can see her receive your number.

High five, you're off to the races! What you say on your first approach should always be a light, brief, two-way conversation, not just you talking. Amusing too, if possible. If she's not responsive, it's totally okay. It's not your fault. Maybe she's late for something. You'll have some practice under your belt. Next!

Now that you've got the initial banter out of the way, it's time to get down to business. No, not that kind of business. I'm talking about signaling to her with your words that you're interested and have what it takes to be a suitable mate.

Understand that until she gets intimate with you, you're on probation. "That sounds harsh." You say? I'm telling it like it is. She'll be on the lookout for potential signs of your not being able to man up. By that I mean be a good father, be strong, protect her, be kind and gentle, and provide for your family. Even if she's very successful and doesn't want kids, this is how women are hardwired.

Craft your introduction carefully. Below are the Fantastic Four essential qualities you must subtly convey to her as your conversation develops:

1. Resources

This could be one or more of the following; note what each one indicates:

- Finances — you are ambitious and successful in what you do for a living.
- Education — you have a decent IQ and discipline and will be able to draw on your schooling to further yourself in life.
- Potential — e.g., you are a talented guitar player, and even if you don't make much money, you still have that potential.

2. Social and Business Status

Best if you have all of these. If you don't, work on it:

- Respect — your peers and friends respect you.
- Leadership — e.g., you're in charge of people at work or socially (team, group).

- Google well — Don't kid yourself, a smart lady will creep on you, I mean sniff you out on Facebook, Google, LinkedIn, etc. You can't hide. She has to do her due diligence and make sure you don't have a family somewhere else!

- Social media presence to show you have a healthy mind and social life.

  - Have 300–800 Facebook friends. Less is anti-social, more is superficial and desperate. (This does not apply to those who use their personal Facebook page for business.)

  - Avoid posting unflattering photos of yourself.

  - Avoid posting overly extreme or judgmental comments.

  - Have a well-written online dating and LinkedIn profile with flattering photos; it shows you care how you present yourself.

  - Take your dating profile down once you start dating her regularly!

- Male friends with whom you spend time.

  - Shows you have what it takes to band together with your comrades to defeat oncoming foes if needed.

3. Physical and Mental Strength

You don't have to be Iron Man or a Mensa member, but it sure helps to be physically and mentally strong and healthy, IQ included:

- Strong quads, buttocks, and arms show her you have the power to sustain physically arduous tasks. It also indicates sexual endurance and versatility with positions. Studies show that women prefer strong men. If that doesn't motivate you to hit the health club ... hmmm.
- Mental and emotional stability matters. We all have our moments but being able to successfully manage them shows willpower and dedication to being a good human being and a great mate.
- Intelligence and being resourceful will get you through life's tricky situations ahead of the pack. Your quick wits will be in high demand with the ladies, partly because more brains tend to beget happier, more stable children. They'll naturally choose to hang with a more successful crowd.
- Confidence and courage showcase your willpower and mental fortitude when you approach her cold. It also shows your respect for and interest in her.

4. Emotional Caring

Even higher than IQ on the dateable scale is EQ (Emotional Quotient). It's the ability to perceive and manage both your emotions and the emotions of others.

You probably have some idea of your IQ, but your awareness of our EQ may be way off:

- EQ in a man is in high demand with women. It tells them you have empathy and can do the paradigm shift. Also, you'll be an understanding, compassionate mate, and father.
- Paradigm shift? Simply put, EQ is the ability to put yourself in another's shoes and understand why they might be behaving the way they are.
- Do you respond to a sticky situation rather than react? There's always a reason for the behavior of others; when you understand the reason, it's often easier to forgive them and respond in an empathic manner instead of dishing it back or reacting with anger.
- Having a higher EQ will get you across her doorstep and into your love life a lot faster.
- Thank goodness you can increase your EQ, and your IQ can be boosted by doing brainwork.

A high EQ goes further than making you better mate material. The *Harvard Business Review* says this about EQ:

> Studies have shown that a high emotional quotient (or EQ) boosts career success, entrepreneurial potential, leadership talent, health, relationship satisfaction, humor, and happiness. It is also the best antidote to work stress and it matters in every job — because all jobs involve dealing with people, and people with higher EQ are more rewarding to deal with.[2]

Having the above four qualities demonstrates discipline and the willpower to succeed. It doesn't get more masculine than that! But how do you put those Fantastic Four into words without sounding boastful or insincere? You weave it into your conversation.

When you build an empathic connection with a woman, you establish an emotional zip-line to her heart.

In the example above, you said this to the sidewalk siren: "Hi, you look like you have great taste. Would you mind helping me out with something, please? I'm looking for a gold bracelet for my little sister's birthday. What jeweler would you recommend? She's turning eighteen, and I want her to have a keepsake from me."

Chick Magnet

Congratulations! You've already indicated that you have three of the Fantastic Four:

- Resources — the money to purchase a gold bracelet.
- Emotional caring — you want you sister to have something special from you to show how much you love her.
- Mental strength — you boldly approached her.

See how easy it is? Now I invite you to come up with some questions you can ask women that show you possess those four qualities. Start talking with her about your feelings and asking her about hers, because when you connect with her in this way, a woman will open up quickly to you.

Look, I understand that, to many of you, the mere thought of talking about your feelings makes you shrivel. But when you open yourself up some and let her see your soft underbelly, you'll see a big difference in how things develop. She'll see you're human and not afraid of being open. You'll build trust because you know you don't need to be perfect. Women communicate on a more emotional level. They're not afraid to talk about their feelings because it's more socially acceptable. That's just how we operate.

When you master the power of showing the chinks in your armor, you'll be way ahead of the pack, you alpha wolf! For men, the "big boys don't cry" attitude is often the norm. I get why it may be hard for you to show your vulnerable side. My parents raised me to be tough and not to cry when I was in pain. It did not serve me well in relationships, because there was no way I was going to tell a boyfriend how he had hurt my feelings! The result was, things never got resolved. He got the cold shoulder, and we'd break up over some stupid misunderstanding.

The quality of my relationships improved vastly once I learned to talk about my feelings and be ok with showing my more vulnerable side to others. In fact, my whole life got better. What I'm getting at is that when a man shows some vulnerability in a paced way, he is showing great strength and courage because he's unafraid of being judged. Peel the onion back slowly, don't go all in too early. Holy frijoles, she's going to love that about you! Men will have more respect for you also. They'll only wish they had your secret sauce to draw in women.

Have you seen a speaker telling a story on stage when, at one point, their voice cracked with emotion? Did you notice how the room fell silent, and every single eyeball fixed on the stage? Like a sci-fi movie where everyone froze except the speaker. Spellbinding. That's the power of vulnerability.

I'm not suggesting you start whining to her how you hate getting up so early or how angry you are with your boss right out of the gate. That'll scare her right out of Dodge. Instead, show Passion and Emotion, not Demotion, when speaking of the things and people you love. Let it show. Let it do its job of conveying your true, brave self.

One of my mentors, Bo Eason, is a master at capturing his audience with the power of personal storytelling. He's an internationally acclaimed coach in high-stakes storytelling and movement.

Bo trains people on using their personal stories to achieve high-impact results. He shares this:

> "The more personal your story is to you, the more influence it's going to have. It's not your company or product they're buying, it's YOU they're buying. It's all you. That's what separates your business from everyone else's. Once you have the structure, then rehearse, rehearse, REHEARSE. You have to refine so it's lean and clean. (Kill your darlings, as the great William Faulkner once said.) If there's no struggle, we're not going to listen."
>
> —Bo Eason

When talking to a woman, be interested and be interesting.

Conversation is an art. It's about finding common ground. You're making a connection and asking her questions about herself to show that you're empathic, kind, courageous and caring. It also helps immensely if you stay abreast of and discuss current affairs, what's trending, the news, etc. You'll quickly find common ground this way.

The key components to having a fruitful conversation with a woman are:

- Ask open-ended questions rather than ones that only require a "yes," "no," "uh-huh" or a yawn.
- Don't offer to fix her problem if she's telling you about one. Women want you to listen to them when they describe a problem they're having. Offering solutions will only frustrate the dickens out of her. End of story. Unless it's a tire she needs changing or something like that...
- Talk less, listen more. We have two ears, one mouth, use them in that 2:1 ratio.
- Listen to her actively. Ask her "How did you feel about that?" It shows interest in her feelings and buys you time to think of your reply by listening to the words she uses.
- Don't interrupt her. Let her finish her sentences. Most men have no idea that they unconsciously interrupt women a lot.
- Turn towards her, look her in the eyes, smile when appropriate.

- Remember her answers. Use them in a later conversation. It's magical to her when you remember what she said.

The #1 complaint from women when we talk about our dating experiences is:

"You know what drives me crazy when I'm on a date? It's when a guy doesn't listen!"

Be a good listener and practice active listening. Look into her eyes, don't interrupt, cock your head slightly now and then, lean in, face her, smile some, nod, say "yes, uh-huh, really? How interesting. That must have made you feel (insert feeling)."

A woman's favorite subject is herself, so ask her questions about herself. When you remember what she said, it will make her feel appreciated. It's the little things that count.

The #2 complaint from women about our first dates is:

"He went on and on about himself, his job, how great he was. What a bore. I was plotting an escape out the bathroom window."

Telling her your life story or a detailed description of your job will have the following effect: Her eyes will start to roll back in her head; she may even begin to foam at the mouth. Some men make this mistake because they're nervous, some make it because they're in the autism spectrum. You do not have to fill every moment of silence with information about yourself. Just ask her about herself. And listen.

The #3 comment on dating is:

"I had to carry the whole conversation. It was exhausting."

Women lose interest when men don't know what to say on a date. This awkward situation becomes disastrous when combined with inappropriate wardrobe. Have a couple of brief anecdotes prepared to share with her if you're stumped on what to say next. Being tongue-tied happens to the best of us.

The solution is to be proactive using this technique:

- Repeat the last few words of her sentence back to her with an interested, inquiring tone. As if you want to hear more. That is exactly what you will get. She will continue and what's more, she'll think you're fascinating!
- For example, she might say "The other day, I saw an eagle fly by." You would then say "An eagle flew by?" She'll then proceed to tell you more.

- Experiment with this. I've used this technique many times and no one was the wiser.

CAUTION: If your date starts spilling her guts about how her ex cheated on her and now he wants custody of the kids, quickly steer the conversation to something neutral. You are not her therapist. Don't even think about discussing her gut-wrenching personal problems with her.

If you do, she will associate you with them and the accompanying emotions; you will thus become a part of the problem. I have dozens of examples on how this has ruined perfectly good relationships. Keep a sharp eye out for this because engaging with her in this way will get you sequestered to the Friend Zone pronto.

Avoid speaking ill of your ex or any other person for that matter. If you do that she'll wonder what you'd say about her should things go south. If she puts others down, walk away. It's a sure sign her issues with him are unresolved or she has poor self-esteem.

Many of us have had harrowing experiences in the past that still haunt us. If this is you, I urge you to seek professional counseling. You're not ready to find love. Keep the talk neutral and positive, and avoid expressing strong opinions until you find out where she stands.

People have different opinions, and she may say things with which you don't agree. That's ok, disagree gently, then move on. You might say "Oh, I see your point, have you thought of looking at it this way?" Or ask "I'm curious, why do you feel that way?"

If you're still struggling with what to say next, notice something interesting she's wearing and ask her to tell you more about it. For instance, you see she's wearing an unusual pair of earrings. You say "I notice your earrings are unique, what's the story behind them?"

She might say "Oh, these? I got them in India." Of course, you can't help but say "In India?" And now you're playing badminton with words! Don't let the birdie touch the ground.

The most important thing you must do besides listening actively and speaking passionately is to be decisive. All women love a confident man with a plan. When you invite her on a date, never, ever expect her to come up with a place to go. The words "I don't know, what do you want to do?" are poison.

You may think you're being a gentleman but she'll think either:

A. You don't like her enough to plan something.

or

B. You're a wishy-washy "yes" man.

Either way your chances of ever seeing her parade around in lacy black lingerie will go straight down the toilet.

YOUR PUNCH LIST

Here's how to transition from yawn-talk into a captivating conversation:

- Skip a beat and engage her in some playful banter first.
- Next, talk about some personal tender moments, passionate moments, joyful moments. (Not ones about former love interests!) Talk about what you love and use the word, love.
- Let that emotion show in your voice, on your face and in your body language.
- Use enthusiasm and passion when you speak — fill her with anticipation and excitement. Monotone is so zzzzzz-zz.
- Now, with that momentum, get your Fantastic Four across.
- Always, always, always ask her about her special moments; coax her to describe them and how she felt.
- Get your foot in the door!

When asking her on a date, always be prepared with the following three strategies:

- Plan A

- Backup plan B
- Backup, backup plan C

As a rule, when presenting a place to go, e.g., a restaurant or a show, give her no more than three options from which to choose. Offering her too many choices will make you appear unsure of your offerings.

The confused mind walks away.

If she changes her mind at the last minute, be cool with it; she has her reasons. You have Plans B & C, and you'll say "Of course, why don't we do this (Plan B) instead." She'll love you for taking charge, taking care of her and knowing exactly what to say!

To build your self image, you need to join the smile, firm handshake and compliment club.

Zig Ziglar

6

FIRST TOUCH

By now you've got a grip on the first telling clues a woman looks for when she initially lays eyes on you. She's seen that you're not a threat and will likely be open to your approach.

You know you're ready to make your first move because:

- You've paid attention to your wardrobe and grooming and have started developing your personal style.
- You've got the basics of powerful yet non-threatening body language.
- When she hears your rich voice, she'll feel immediately drawn in, and she'll want to hear more because you sound confident and trustworthy.
- You're able to capture her attention and make her feel like she's the only one in the room with the eye contact you've practiced.

Now it's time to take the plunge; you're going to reach out and touch her for the first time. Keep your shorts on. Once you get this simple technique under your belt, you'll be way ahead of the others.

It's a huge step; I'm talking about the handshake. The way you shake her hand will either make her immediately want to know more about you or, horrors... will get you out of the arena and onto the bleachers.

But before you touch her hand, you've got to let her ears hear your voice. You're asking for permission to touch her by using the vibration of your voice. You're not actually saying "Ok if I touch you?" You're just letting her hear your voice first. It's a split-second thing, but it has a significant impact in making her feel comfortable

Follow these steps in order of appearance:

- Say "Hi, my name is ______." The sound of your manly voice has a vibration and is the first thing that enters her body.
- Your hand should already be reaching out, but your voice has to make contact with her senses first.
- Smile warmly with both your eyes and your mouth.

Compare, if you will, the handshake to the hug. If you're a hugger, you'll know what I'm talking about. Are you familiar with the A-frame hug? I've got one word to describe that one: Ugh! It's is where the other person only touches you with their shoulders; it's as if you have a terminal armpit flea infestation. You might even get a pat on the back to terminate the hug.

The bigger the pat, the more uncomfortable the other person is. Their reluctance to make physical contact is palpable. Doesn't it make you wonder if they've noticed the fleas and can't wait until it's over?

Now, remember the person who gave you that full-frontal wraparound hug, pressing their heart to yours for just a wee second longer than most people do. Not too soft, not too hard, just the right amount of squeeze. Okay, personally I'm a big fan of bear hugs. I love those kinds of hugs because they are sincere and unapologetic. It tells me th

at I'm accepted and appreciated by the hugger.

That's the kind of person I want to spend more time with, and I'm sure most women do too! Take that analogy and apply it to a handshake. Your handshake should be firm enough to let her know you're sure of yourself but not crushing.

Let's take a look at the three most common handshakes:

1. **The Death Grip**

An overly firm handshake is only useful if you want to get rid of someone. My Russian friend Nikolai used this technique to deter a fellow who was making inappropriate advances on his girlfriend, Jennifer, at the beach one summer. Measuring in at 6 foot, 5 inches and 250 lbs. of solid muscle, Nikolai had been on Russia's national bobsled team. His mitts were sizable enough to envelop most people's hands.

When Jennifer told him about the unwelcome suitor, Nikolai sauntered over and, with a smile introduced himself with a long handshake so "firm" that the offending bloke begged for mercy. He never bothered Jennifer again! Only crush if you're tall and muscular and you're particularly fond of your girlfriend.

2. **The Limp Fish**

On the other hand, a weak handshake from a man will immediately have a woman wondering if he's weak. You know the kind of handshake I'm referring to, where the person's hand is a limp fish?

When I get the limp handshake from a client, I'll always ask for the reason behind their "barely there" grip. The answer I most often get is, "When I was growing up my dad told me to be extra gentle when shaking a lady's hand, so I don't hurt her." They were told to touch a woman's fingers from the knuckles down only, and — "whatever you do, son, don't squeeze too hard or too long."

Did your mom ever tell you to treat a lady's hand like a fragile flower? I didn't think so. It's the last thing a mother would say to her son. Women are not as frail as you may think and will presume you lack in masculinity and chutzpah if your handshake treats her like she's made of glass. You've got to give it some oomph!

Related to the limp fish handshake is the wet fish handshake. It's understandable to think having sweaty palms might betray your shaky nerves to attractive women. It's normal, and you know what? Women get sweaty palms too; we just never tell you. Clammy hands can easily be forgiven if combined with a confident "Hello," suitable body language, direct eye contact and above all, a firm grip.

Give her a limp and clammy fish, and it's over. No one wants to touch that. You have to give her hand a good squeeze no matter the sogginess of your palms. If she sees you're nervous she'll appreciate the courage it took you to approach her. She'll know it means a lot to you.

3. **The Two-Handed Pump**

There's another type of handshake that'll also have her backing away from you. I call it the two-handed pump. It's is when a guy envelops a woman's hand with both of his hands, pumps and then doesn't let go.

When this happens, she'll get the impression that he's desperate, smothering and worried that she'd vamoose the minute he releases her hand; which is exactly what she might do. She'll want her hand back pronto because this kind of grip is overbearing and makes her feel trapped.

It's okay if you gently and briefly rest your other hand on top of hers for one second but not for the entire shake. It will garner a touch more of her attention. But be careful not to hold on too long, or you'll be skating on thin ice.

The Just Right Shake

My papa took a person's handshake very seriously. To him, it was an indication of their integrity, honesty, and self-assurance. He wasn't far off; You can derive so much information from just a handshake. I'm forever thankful for the valuable handshake lesson he taught my brother and me when we little kids. He shared why it was important, and then he'd practice with us. His technique has served me well.

When shaking hands, make sure the webbing between your forefinger and thumb meets the other person's. It says "I'm here and I've got nothing to hide" both literally and figuratively. Are you wondering "How long should my handshake last?" What a great question because it matters! The answer is 1 to 2 seconds, no less, no more.

Making eye contact is essential before, during and after your handshake. It respectfully shows you're paying attention to the person. Jittery nerves can make this a real challenge to some like Mike, with the "butterfly chasing" eyes. You have it in you to make yourself do this. Remember the 66-day rule to create new habits? You deserve to succeed in love.

I understand how unnatural it can feel for those with Asperger's to make eye contact. If this is you, please do your best to practice it because it's considered rude to look away when shaking hands. Others will interpret it as, "I'll shake your hand because I have to, but you're not worthy of my attention."

The quality of your handshake is not to be understated because it will convey your confidence and willpower. It's your very first skin-to-skin contact and tells others you know who you are and that you're capable.

Your display of physical strength and your ability to use it in a measured way tells her that you're able to defend her should a tribe of Konyak headhunter warriors ambush you. If you offer her a limp fish handshake, she'll wonder "Yikes, does he think he only has to run faster than me?"

If you want a woman to consider you as a possible date or mate rather than a dud, you've got to master the handshake. By the way, this technique will get you taken more seriously at work and socially as well because it's a universal telltale indicator of your self-esteem and courage.

Yes, I said courage! Any person with integrity will recognize how Herculean it can be for some to conquer their jittery nerves and negative self-talk. The efforts you're making to be your best are appreciated and will pay off. I promise.

The skin, the largest organ in our body, covers about 20 square feet. It's the most complex organ in the somatosensory system (sense of touch) and is the first barrier protecting us from the outside environment.

A study by Matt Hertenstein, an experimental psychologist at DePauw University in Indiana reveals that touching another person in a friendly way — such as a handshake, hand-holding or hugging — does two things:

1. Decreases the stress hormone cortisol, creating a calming effect
2. Increases release of oxytocin — also called the "cuddle hormone" — which affects trust behaviors.

Oxytocin is a neuropeptide, which basically promotes feelings of devotion, trust and bonding," Hertenstein says. The cuddle hormone makes us feel close to one another. It really lays the biological foundation and structure for connecting to other people.

Besides engendering feelings of closeness, being touched is also pleasant. We usually want more. So what's going on in the brain that accounts for these feelings?

The surging of oxytocin makes you feel more trusting and connected. And the cascade of electrical impulses slows your heart and lowers your blood pressure, making you feel

> less stressed and more soothed. Remarkably, this complex surge of events in the brain and body are all initiated by a simple, supportive touch.[3]

A simple handshake done right will make her relax and feel good. The cool thing is that it will simultaneously do the same for you. And that's only the first touch! An introductory handshake is a fantastic, socially acceptable way to introduce a woman to your touch. It's is the very first chunk of ice you'll break when you want to connect with a woman. It sets the cornerstone for further physical interaction. Your next physical move will be that much easier because you've introduced her to you physically. You've already touched her. It's set in her mind and body now; she's felt you. So make it a good handshake.

If giving a woman a firmer handshake is not something you're accustomed to, you'll feel like you're invasive at first. Move past that feeling post-haste because first impressions are very hard to fix after the fact.

If it's too late, here's what it'll take to fix it:

Be persistent...

- If you're determined to win someone over after a rough start, be warned that your efforts may take some time. "A Harvard study suggests that it will take eight subsequent positive encounters to change that person's negative opinion of you. In this context be "persistent and patient," reports leadership specialist Roz Usheroff.[4]

... and consistent

- While a sustained effort over time may be required to change an unfavorable first impression, it's not sufficient. You also need to be stable in your subsequent behavior. Counselor and coach Susan Fee cautions: "Overcoming a bad impression requires that all future behavior be consistent with how you want to be perceived."[5]

Practice, Practice, Practice

When my papa said "You've got to shake hands like you mean it," he meant "make your presence known in no uncertain terms." Women should shake hands the same way.

Here's a recap of the winning handshake:

- Keep it firm even if your hands are clammy. Clammy hands are forgivable; a limp handshake is not.
- Maintain eye contact before, during and after the handshake to show her she has your full attention.

- Keep the entire length of the shake around 1-1.5 seconds. Longer is desperate, shorter is fearful.
- Use just one hand. A two-handed grip is possessive, especially when coupled with an extra long grip. It makes the recipient feel trapped and want to bolt.

Every cell in your body might resist this method because it counters the habits and beliefs you may have been raised with. Maybe it was well-intentioned advice from your dad, or perhaps no one ever took the time to show you the ropes.

If you're thinking, "No, can't do it, this doesn't feel right, and I've never done it this way. It's too much, and I'm afraid it's going to backfire," it's too late. It's already going wrong. Start creating the new handshake habit now because it'll showcase your confidence to others, and it'll build yours.

Practice is required to wrap your muscle memory around this vital technique, Remember that the skill set taught in this book will take some time to absorb. When you do each technique for 66 days, they become habits.

Just like learning a new language, you must practice with others and keep doing so until it all becomes second nature. If you don't exercise those muscles, you'll lose the language.

You'll need to introduce yourself to others to work on your handshake technique. Start by introducing yourself to at least one new person every day. Make it your business to attend events, seminars, community gatherings, the gym, etc. Scan the room and select one or two people. It's easy if you find yourself sitting or standing next to someone at a gathering— just introduce yourself to them! Anywhere there are people; you can practice.

If you're socially awkward like my friend Greg, do what he does. He makes it a point to introduce himself to one new person each day and hold a brief conversation with them. He favors senior citizens because they're so appreciative and often ignored. You'll be amazed how warm and fuzzy you'll feel for doing a good deed. It'll be written all over your face, and that, my friend, will make you very appealing to women.

After shaking someone's hand, you'll automatically be at the right distance from them for initial conversation. In North America, this distance is about 3 feet, unless you're in a crowded room. Once you're comfortable executing this with women you're not romantically interested in, move on to the ones you find attractive.

It's essential that you make the first move to introduce yourself to a woman. It's is your opportunity to disarm her with your eye contact, smile, confident, relaxed voice and oh, let's not forget your impressive handshake. First touch, done!

How could she not let her guard down and smile back at you? So far you've done all the right things to show you're interested in her as a person and that you're friendly and confident. Maybe she didn't know anybody in the room either and is relieved to have someone to talk to.

Be social. Introduce yourself to the newbie. Make a new friend.

If being in a room full of strangers is daunting for you, do a paradigm shift. Put yourself in the other people's shoes. Remind yourself that others may be feeling the same as you. Turn it around and act as if you're the host. Be of service to them by saying "welcome!" They'll quickly feel comfortable around you, and you'll be pleasantly surprised at how many wonderful new friends you make! In fact, should you run into these folks again, they're very likely to seek you out because of the way you made them feel.

Introducing yourself to someone in this way conveys that you recognize them as a fellow human being. You're welcoming them and thanking them for being here in this chance encounter. It always makes a person feel good about themselves. Bonus points for you.

YOUR PUNCH LIST

Introducing yourself to strangers is a form of acknowledgment. It's very welcoming. Here are the steps; follow them in this order:

- Make eye contact. Maintain it as you approach the person, during the handshake and afterward. Keep your head up. Do not look at the ground.

- Smile. Always start with a small smile and let it grow on your face as you approach.
- Say "Hi, my name is ______". If the other person doesn't offer their name, ask their name after saying yours. Start speaking a split second before you reach out your hand.
- Shake their hand for 1–2 second with just the right firmness, using the web-to-web grip.

What do you say we start a movement to bring back the handshake? We need more human contact and much less cell phone contact.

Do it like a gentleman. Get out there and start shakin' it!

Don't take yourself so damn seriously!

Dr. Wayne Dyer

7

THE SEXIEST QUALITY OF ALL

Scene 1: You're at a party, lying in wait for just the right moment to go chat up Ms Hot Stuff and here it is; she's finally alone! You try to convince yourself you've got this but the nauseating swarm of butterflies in your stomach has your feet nailed to the floor. Or was it that Jack and Coke you just chugged talking back? You pry your feet loose and wobble over to her praying, "Please don't let me spew on her. I promise I'll never drink again."

Scene 2: You're cruising down the highway when you see an oncoming 18-wheeler cross over the double line and right into your path. At that life-and-death moment, an ice hot surge of energy shocks through your body and instantaneously makes you swerve out of death's way. That prickly surge just saved your life.

Both these reactions are caused by your nervous system signaling danger to the limbic brain, aka "lizard brain," when danger is perceived. This fight or flight response happens not only for physical but also emotional danger. Adrenalin shoots through your body like someone just injected your veins with electrified ice water. Your body immediately reacts and makes you either spew or swerve.

Hopefully you'll never experience Scene 2, but Scene 1 happens to most of us at some point. It happened to Louis, a successful businessman — handsome, confident, popular, always smiling. Most women would describe him as a good catch. When I was photographing him for his online dating profile, he revealed something very personal to me.

We had just wrapped the shoot when I asked him, "How's the dating going?"

"Well, actually, I have no problem having a conversation with women I'm not attracted to. But when I see a pretty woman to whom I *am* attracted, I get so nervous and tongue-tied, my palms get all sweaty and I just can't do it," said Louis. "Why do you get nervous?" I asked. "Because I figure she gets hit on constantly and she'll just turn me down," he replied. Wow, that hit a button for me. There's a myth I want to bust about that limiting belief.

Louis's perception about beautiful women getting hit on constantly is simply not true. In fact, during my former career as a professional fashion model, I was just as nervous as Louis was. Paradoxically, it was guys like Louis that I wanted to date because they made me feel so good about myself. The hunky male models I dated usually left me feeling empty, and I was hungry for true love. The cover boys didn't have to try as hard because women would flock to them. It's a pity that the Louis types were afraid to ask me out because of that silly old myth they believed. Imagine all the fun we could've had!

Well, the bad news is: The nerves and adrenalin will always be there because your life could depend on it. The good new is: You can control how you respond to the fight or flight urge. Look, your limbic system is engineered to protect you. The problem is that it can't differentiate between life-threatening danger and the fear of getting turned down by Ms. Hot Stuff.

So how do you change your mindset? You need to be even more afraid of *failing* to go for it when you want to talk to Ms. Hot Stuff.

Make fear of failure part of what fuels your desire to succeed.

When I started modeling I had pretty low self-esteem. Okay, the truth is I was terrified. But what scared me more was the thought that I'd hate myself if I didn't push forward. I challenged myself to unchain the confident woman that was inside of me. Becoming a model frightened me so much it made me want to vomit. That's why I chose that career.

On the morning of a big photo shoot I'd be so anxious the sound of my pounding heart beat like a timpani drum inside my head. I thought I would expire! As a result I spent a lot of time preparing for the worst-case scenario. Somehow this always greatly improved my performance. My overactive nerves gradually became accustomed to the rhythm of this systematic preparation. They calmed down. I gained more and more confidence and began to practice having playful, teasing conversations, or banter, with the others on set. Feeling anxious about blowing it and getting fired actually gave me the courage to charge forward and take the risk! As a bonus, the banter also served to make me more popular.

While starting a conversation comes naturally to some people, many men, and women too, get very antsy at the thought of it. As a bit of an introvert, being in a room full of people was tortuous for me until I learned how to start a conversation with anyone using what I call playful banter.

I perfected this technique one evening with help from Grant, a friend who'd been the lead coach at a one of the original self-development programs in London, England. We were attending a networking event together in the lounge of my business club. The atmosphere was lively and well attended, but since I didn't see many familiar faces I felt awkward. I was afraid that strangers would try to talk to me. What the dickens would we talk about? I turned to Grant to suggest we grab a glass of wine but, poof, he had disappeared. Help! I made my way to belly up the bar to so I'd at least have one side of me protected.

Finally I spotted him in the middle of the room leaning down and chatting to a group of three women who were enjoying appetizers at a table. They were already engrossed in a friendly conversation. When he was done chatting up the ladies, he joined me at the bar, to which my back was now crazy-glued. "Did you know those ladies?" I queried. It was curious because I thought this was his first time at the club.

Grant replied, "No, not at all, but when I enter a room full of people I don't know, I always go and talk to someone right away. That breaks the ice because if I wait, I start to feel nervous and left out."

Who knew? What a perfect way to avert the "jam-packed room jitters." Just jump in straight away and go talk to someone before your palms go clammy. You'll have already met the first person and made them feel welcome!

If you suffer from the jitters, I highly recommend using this technique. It's one of the smartest things you can do in such a situation because guess what? It will boost your confidence in a jiffy since you were the one who initiated the contact. The bonus is that you also made the other person feel special.

It's so much more effective than waiting for people to come up to you. You know the feeling you get when you attend say, a networking event alone? If you're a bit reserved, you'll standing there by yourself clutching a drink in front of you like a shield, pretending you're looking for someone. You bloody well know there's no one you know there, which makes you feel utterly unpopular.

This is the time to turn it into a game and find someone entertaining to hang out with, man or woman, and practice your bantering skills. You could pick up a trick or two. Have some fun — enthusiasm is contagious. The big thing on approach is that it should be natural and real — even better if it can be witty, but it doesn't have to be.

Always punch above your weight.

It's a conundrum, and now you know how to get over the hump fast. Do it cold turkey, dive in, and don't even think about it. Scan the crowd as you enter the room, and immediately head over to someone (preferably in a small group of mostly women). Introduce yourself to one of the ladies, and with a smile ask her a question like, "When does the show start?" Even if there's no show,

just assume you know something she doesn't. Be playful!

Most likely she'll smile, you'll all introduce yourselves, and bingo! You're part of the group, and now have a conversation going. Not only that, but you look like you belong. Secretly, most people would love to speak up and be entertaining, but many are too intimidated or introverted. So when you jump in like this, you're already a cut above — people see that and you have their attention. Once you get used to this practice, it will become second nature even if you normally feel awkward in social settings.

My first year in college I didn't know anyone, so I'd drive around on weekend nights with my brother looking for house parties. Most such parties would have a beer keg somewhere. Once we found one that was going full blast, I'd stroll in first and ask, "Have you seen Mike?" Of course I didn't know any Mike there, but it was a safe bet there'd be at least three of them in the house. My next question would be, "Where's the keg?" In a flash we were "in" because I knew Mike, and now we knew where the keg was. Sneaky but it worked!

Moving up the ladder, the Playful Banter technique (not the beer keg one) is extremely useful when you want to be perceived as popular. It's a hugely important factor with the ladies because it shows them you've got healthy social skills. You're not the "nice quiet guy who kept to himself and then blew up the neighborhood."

Here's the how-to:

- Slowly saunter in, walking tall, and scan the room.
- Spot a group of about three people or so, preferably including two women.
- Walk over to them with a pleasant expression on your face. Use a confident steady gaze, head held high.
- Make eye contact, smile, shake hands with and introduce yourself to the least attractive.

- Next, ask her a playful question.
- Chat for no more than 15 to 20 seconds with her.
- She may already be in a relationship, and a lengthy first banter will make her think you're hitting on her.
- Now introduce yourself to the others. It's impolite to monopolize one person when first meeting a group.

This technique can easily be used as well in casual social settings, like a party. I recommend this to you because it kills three birds with one stone:

1. It's a great warmup to moving on to that intriguing raven-haired beauty standing by the fridge.
2. It tells other women you are not a threat.
3. You break the ice by demonstrating a light-hearted, easy-to-be-with character. You've made someone smile!

The reason you're going up to the least attractive woman first is to show that you are not a desperate hound. I'm serious, this works!

Women have eyes in the backs of their heads. That's why they make such great moms. They also generally have keener intuitive powers than men do. Sniffing out trouble is their business. Like a Green Beret landing in enemy territory, any woman worth her salt will always use situational awareness in a social environment. If Ms Hot Stuff notices you're not immediately hitting on the obvious competition, she'll know you're not a hound.

If, on the other hand, you look like you're shopping all the pretty girls in the room one by one, she'll be turned off. She'll feel unsafe because you appear to be a pick up artist on the prowl. No self-respecting woman wants to be a part of that game.

Feel free to approach a few groups this way as it helps you build extra confidence. Also, continue to ask more questions of the group, like "How do you know each other?" or "Do you like disco music? I'm conducting a poll." It can absolutely be a silly question. Making someone smile or laugh helps dissipate any awkward or uncomfortable moment. A woman will want to spend more time with a man who makes her laugh and feel comfortable.

Once you've done the initial ice-breaking by talking to groups, what's next? Now you're primed and ready to approach the gal you've had your eye on since you first walked in. Make it your focus to have her feeling comfortable and appreciated around you. Remember, she's probably feeling just as nervous as you. Relax her with your introduction and a little playful exchange of words. Look at you, you've officially started flirting with her!

Keep your eyes on hers; don't let your gaze wander. No matter if a pair of jeans walks by looking like 10 pounds of sugar stuffed in a 5 pound bag. That's what peripheral vision is for. These first few moments of contact with her shape the first impression you give her. Make it count by paying attention to her and making her smile and laugh. Ask her questions about herself, tease her a little. Play. Many a mother has looked their daughter straight in the eyes and asked, "Does he make you laugh? If he can make you laugh, that's a good sign."

If you're still hesitating to approach her, ask yourself, "What's the worst thing that could happen?" If she turns you down your life has not changed one iota other than you've just gotten more valuable practice in. You are free to move, excuse yourself and find someone who appreciates you. Your person/people are there, just keep looking.

Be sure to maintain a "glass half full" mindset. Stick to positive topics. One of the biggest turn-offs for women is a man who criticizes others and complains a lot. Keep it light, fun and playful.

A good sense of humor is a great confidence asset because it makes you a joy to be around. You make people feel good. Caution: Avoid over-using self-depreciating humor. It will be interpreted as a lack of confidence. She'll think, "If he doesn't value himself, why should I?" Humility is another valuable confidence asset. It's not about groveling or low self-esteem; it's an intentionally powerful state of mind. It's knowing your own personal power and yet always being able to engage the other person with a humble inquiry.

Chick Magnet

"Humble Inquiry: The fine art of drawing someone out, of asking questions to which you do not already know the answer, of building a relationship based on curiosity and interest in the other person."

— Edgar H. Schein

Let's say you've just noticed a woman with mesmerizing green eyes standing in line right in front of you at the coffee shop and, ugh, you feel that sickening knot in your stomach. Your imagination whirls with thoughts of you and her enjoying a passionate weekend on a tropical beach, waves lapping at your thighs as you embrace. Wake up! You're already Photoshopping her into your life, and you haven't even said hello. While visualizing is a useful tool, if you're already hesitant to make your initial approach, fantasizing like this will trip you up. You just want to say, "Hello," not "Hello, will you have my children?"

While the beach vacation certainly is a desirable outcome, at this point a full-blown romantic fantasy will amplify the pressure and cause a train wreck. Plus who knows if she's even available? You've got so much energetic momentum that you're about to burst into flames! Breathe. Deeply. Three times. If you approach her with flames in your eyes, your anxiety will be written all over your face. It'll even make her feel nervous, and that's the exact opposite of what you want. The objective is to make her feel comfortable, safe and joyful around you. Be that confident friendly protector. "But how?" you wonder? I'm so glad you asked! There's a technique to this. Since you can't quell the flood of fear, use your energetic momentum to convert it into a different, equally intense emotion — excitement. Think of it as energy in motion. Whatever you do, don't stop feeling the excitement. Put a smile on your face, adopt a confident posture and move your energy towards that pretty woman. One foot in front of the other, Braveheart.

> "Are you paralyzed with fear? That's a good sign. Fear is good. Like self-doubt, fear is an indicator. Fear tells us what we have to do. Remember one rule of thumb: the more scared we are of a work or calling, the more sure we can be that we have to do it."
>
> — Steven Pressfield, *The War of Art*

Here's the technique broken down:

- Take a long, deep, letting go breath; your brain desperately needs oxygen right now. Exhale.
- Make your move quickly, just like you did when you practiced talking to small groups of people. Hesitating will only feed your resistance and cause an intestinal butterfly convention.
- Lift the corners of your mouth and say something like, "Hi, let me guess. You're a latte lover, right?"
- Keep it casual and upbeat, whatever you say.

- You have the advantage of already being in her physical proximity because you're in line; use it!

Another great way to strike up a conversation is to do it while you are moving. Ever notice how much easier it is to talk to someone while you're doing something physical, such as driving or walking? Approaching someone while you're in motion helps dissipate some of the nervous energy you may be feeling. My stunning friend Kate was walking down a city street when she saw two guys walking in her direction. They were chatting and joking with one another. As they neared, one of them stopped her and asked, "Excuse me, do women prefer cabernet or pinot?" It totally caught her off guard. It was clear he was trying to pick her up, but he did it in a charming, non-threatening way. She had two options: answer the question and move on or engage in further conversation. Her choice. It was all done in good humor, and she felt no expectations or pressure. This way nobody lost face. Practice this technique using different questions when you're out with a buddy. Challenge each other and have fun with it!

Building your confidence level takes effort but the rewards are myriad. You'll stop feeling starved for love because you'll love *yourself* more. Now that's an attractive quality that'll have confidence oozing from every pore! Singles who are starved emotionally and financially often have low self-esteem. This can only attract co-dependent relationships. Flourish independently and you'll attract a woman who is your equal. This is a non-negotiable ingredient for a lasting, healthy relationship.

Fill your life with things that make you happy and build your confidence socially. Have fun with your guy friends. Your buddies are your support system. Oh, and it's a turn-on when women see you having good times with your friends. She'll see a man who has social capital and is sure of himself.

YOUR PUNCH LIST

Here are some places to practice you bantering skills with women:

- Volunteer somewhere where your preferred kind of woman is also likely to volunteer, e.g., church, homeless shelter, boys and girls club, Rotary Club, etc. You'll showcase your emotional caring perfectly this way.
- Attend improv classes. I can't say enough about this. This'll skyrocket your quick-wittedness and ability to drum up humorous conversation.
- Join Toastmasters, learn how to converse concisely and confidently.
- Join social clubs and meet-ups that revolve around your interests.

- Join a co-ed team sports activity such as volleyball, a rowing club or tennis club. Something you genuinely enjoy.

You'll feel good about doing good, and that both builds confidence and reduces fear. Remember to keep these activities to ones that you actually like. No faking an interest in underwater basket-weaving just to get the girl. She'll sniff you out in a New York Minute. Of course you're on the prowl. But to make this work for you, step into the arena your most authentic, relaxed, confident, playful self.

Whatever happens on this journey, you're going to love yourself for doing it. And so will she!

There is nothing so electric as that first touch.

8

PHYSICAL TOUCH

You've engaged her in conversation, and you can tell from her body language she's feeling relaxed. You've mastered the technique of making her eyes flash with mirth. You do it efficiently and often because you now know that laughter is a surefire way to make her whole body release tension and doubt. The verbal rapport you've initiated has her feeling emotionally connected with you. Bingo! Her guard is down, and she's opening up to you. All this in one brief conversation ... yet the risk of falling into the Friend Zone still lurks in the shadows. What will it take to tip things in your favor?

It's is the moment where you convey your romantic interest in her. It's time to touch her, again. Hopefully, you've already done the handshake, and that's a perfect start. We're taking it up a notch now. Relax, I'm not suggesting you place the palm of your hand on her sweet derrière, you naughty boy!

Scientists say that skin contact causes the brain to release a flood of neuropeptides called oxytocin, aka the bonding hormone. It also causes levels of the stress hormone cortisol to drop.

"A soft touch on the arm makes the orbital frontal cortex light up," says Matt Hertenstein, an experimental psychologist at DePauw University in Indiana. The surging of oxytocin makes you feel more trusting and connected. And the cascade of electrical impulses slows your heart and lowers your blood pressure, making you feel less stressed and more soothed. Remarkably, this complex surge of events in the brain and body are all initiated by a simple, supportive touch."

Since touch is an even more powerful stimulus for women than it is for men, you must use it wisely. Touching her the wrong way at this stage will set off an alarm inside her body. Touching her the right way is entirely acceptable and desired when you're speaking with her. It's surprising how many men avoid touching because they were brought up to think that it is verboten to touch a woman during casual conversation.

This idea arose during the period of industrialization. Ever since the mass movement away from rural to urban areas to seek better-paying work, fathers have spent their days at the office or factory and not with their boys working the farm. Consequently, boys ended up being taught life lessons and raised primarily by women. It was their mothers and their teachers who naturally taught their sons by example how to think and act. So these boys grew up with female role models and had less and less contact and with father figures.

Many misconceptions of how to be a man were born of this phenomenon. We now have a world of "Mr. Nice Guys" who must reclaim their manhood by adopting the more alpha male behavior that naturally attracts women. Once a man learns why not touching her will keep him in the Friend Zone, he'll wisely make it his business to adjust his childhood blueprint. By determining the right touching points and employing the other techniques taught within these pages, he'll kiss the Friend Zone bye-bye. The Nice Guys are missing out on all the delightful benefits of oxytocin, quelle horreur!

The best and most appropriate way to touch is by just using the back of your hand to lightly and briefly touch a lady's upper arm when making a point. Just enough so she feels it, but not too hard or too long to make her feel threatened. It's a dance. To do this, you will have to move in a little bit closer to her side than when you first introduced yourself.

When meeting that luscious redhead, you most likely started by facing her, maybe shaking her hand and remained at roughly the same distance while talking. That's fine if you're only planning to do business with her, but don't you have more on your mind than that?

Here's how to move closer:

- When you offer your hand, make a mental note of the distance between you.
- Briefly engage in a little banter in this 1st position (see diagram below).
- When you notice she's feeling relaxed, step into 2nd position.
- Position yourself at a 45° angle to one side of her, and at half the original distance.
- You're now closer, but since you're no longer facing her full frontal, she still feels safe.

- Now it feels more natural to give her that little back of the hand tap on the upper arm.

- Don't overdo it; a little goes a long way.

Since women are more affected by raised oxytocin levels from being touched, they'll already start to feel good and trust you more the minute you touch them in this non-threatening way. An interesting tidbit is that women will feel the loving, trusting after-effects of oxytocin for two weeks. Men on the other hand only enjoy the warm and fuzzy feeling for two days.

Here's the secret to why the oxytocin tidbit is so significant: A prospective lover who likes you will feel miffed when you don't reach out to her for a whole week after the first date.

Big Tip:

- **If you want to see her again, call her within two days before the cuddle drug supply dries up!**

A woman's most powerful sex organ is her brain. That is where the whole mating dance starts, and if she feels at all imperiled by you, it's over. Women are different from men that way.

Pssst ... when you touch us the right way it can send shivers down our spine. Don't tell anyone I told you that!

Use your imagination and think of other great ways to briefly touch her. It'll get her mind thinking about getting more. Create opportunities to get within touching range of her. Consider sitting at the adjacent side of the table rather than across from your date. A perfect time to make physical contact with her is when she's laughing. You lean in, say something funny, and you're both laughing — it's totally fine to touch her arm or shoulder.

Here are some other suggestions to get you started:

- Never let your hand slip to below her waist when using this technique. That's below the belt and will scare her off.
- You may place the palm and fingers of your hand lightly on her upper back when:
- Guiding her over to another spot in the room
- Guiding her over to a table
- Showing her through a doorway
- Introducing her to someone you know
- Asking her if she'd like a drink
- When seated together at a table you might gently touch the top of her hand briefly to make a point

It can seem harmless to playfully touch a damsel's posterior at a party after a couple of drinks, but it can destroy your chances of ever getting near her again. She has boundaries and will expect you to observe them.

The bottom line, however, is proximity and situational awareness. You might be standing so close in a crowded room that the back of your hand comes in contact with her thigh. Don't stroke her leg, just let things stand as if it's accidental. If she's uncomfortable, she'll either turn or move away. So be patient, move toward the goal and monitor everything. Essentially, this is foreplay, and you're learning what your new friend is comfortable with.

While at a summer gala affair in a ritzy neighborhood I had something like this happen. The champagne was flowing, and I was wearing a form-fitting silk dress. While chatting with a couple of people I suddenly I felt a hand stroke my rear. I stopped in mid-sentence and wheeled around to confront the perp. I saw it was Mick, a man I knew. He gleefully chuckled, "I'm checking all the girls to see who's wearing a g-string."

Since then he's been crossed off my list. The word is out in town because I've warned all my female friends about him. Had this happened at an office party, he would have lost his job. The sad thing is that Mick probably was so hammered he doesn't even remember his grope. He looks puzzled every time he gets the cold shoulder from me. Being inebriated is no excuse for crude behavior.

If I had it do again, he would be wearing my drink. It pays to keep a clear head when out on the hunt. Numbing your senses from the approach anxiety also numbs your sense of propriety.

Every woman I know has been subject to at least one unwelcome sexual encounter from a man who was inebriated, and probably many more. The first thought that enters my mind when faced with an intoxicated "hello" is to move away from that hot mess as quickly as possible. I know he's quite likely to touch me inappropriately. It's how a sanguine woman will protect herself from what might happen. And that is precisely the kind of woman I want for you.

Her impression of an inebriated approach turns from curiosity to "He can't possibly respect himself or me to be talking to me in this condition." Even if she met him through friends, he would have to start from scratch to overwrite this new impression. The trust between them would self-destruct because, to a woman, a drunk man is a dangerous man.

Whatever sex appeal the man may initially possess vanishes into his alcohol-laden breath. Even a man who holds his liquor well cannot escape the effect that alcohol and other substances have on the amount of blood flow to erectile tissue. Rather a wilting thought.

A little libation is fine but keep in mind that your goal is to be intoxicating, not intoxicated.

It's important to observe a maiden's body language before you consider touching her, aside from the harmless handshake, of course. What I mean by that is don't rush in too soon to touch her — she will feel threatened. It's like a dance in this initial stage, except for now she is leading. If she's a business colleague, avoid any touching outside of a handshake. Don't dip your pen in the company ink.

At first you must mirror her body language. Did I just hear you think "What!? I should adjust my bra strap and fluff my hair?" No need to go that far, but mirroring will help establish a connection with her. It's an effective technique used to build trust and understanding quickly. When she sees her reflection in you she'll automatically think "Hey, there's something I like about this guy."

Avoid mirroring any negative body language because she'll think you've got bad vibes. Here are some examples of how this works:

Her body language:	**Do mirror if she's:**	**Don't mirror if she's:**
Posture	Leaning on something	Slouching
Sitting position	Leaning in to you	Leaning away, stay neutral
Legs crossed	Crossing legs toward you	Crossing legs away

Her voice:	Do mirror if it's:	Don't mirror if it's:
pitch	Low to mid-ranged	Nasal or high-pitched
Pace	Speaking at slow or medium speed	Speaking rapidly
Tone	Happy	Angry
Volume	Comfortably audible	Overly loud or barely audible
Melody	Varied	Monotone

Remember to wear your smile!

Whatever you do, don't move in too fast with your body. If you notice even the smallest sign of her turning or moving away from you, back off. Hopefully she trusts you enough by now to stick around and maybe give you another chance. Like I said before, it's a dance, a *pas de deux*.

The other reason you'll want to follow her lead at first is that you've got to give a gal time to absorb you, drink you in. It's not that women don't want you to touch them, quite the opposite. Touching the right way helps build a physical connection between the two of you. It's also another way of showing her you're paying extra attention to her and that you want *her* attention. When you give attention the right way, you get attention in return.

During this phase you have to be particularly aware of your companion's responses to your touch. Did she reciprocate and touch you back? Did she pull away? Watch as the dance gets progressively more exciting, and perhaps risky. But oh boy. Once it starts, it's like a drug. Can I have some more please?

Using the numerous techniques we've covered to get her full attention now turns into stimulating her physical realm. Her sense of touch is now activated, making the possibility of more touching a natural progression. You are paving the way for your fist kiss!

Be sure to only feed your touch to her bit by bit. If she likes you, she'll want more. Her anticipation of what might happen next is already becoming foreplay for her. It's part of the flirting game, and she wants to savor it. Just like a delicious piece of gourmet chocolate, you let it sit on your tongue for a while. It slowly warms up and melts, filling your senses with its flavor and aroma, mmm-mmm. You resist the urge to bite hard and devour it too fast.

Have you ever visited someone's house who had a cat? If you're an animal lover and have introvert tendencies, you might lean down to pet Miss Meow first to help break the ice. You know what's likely to happen when you move in a little too fast. Ms. Kitty backs away because she's apprehensive of your intentions. She might even go hide behind her human's leg and eye you

with suspicion, tail switching side to side. You'd think she was a scaredy cat, right?

If, on the other hand, you go down on your haunches and extend your finger for her to sniff, it's a different story. She then lets you carefully stroke her on the side of her cheek. Play your cards right, and she'll be jumping in your lap and begging for more.

YOUR PUNCH LIST

Here's how to play your petting cards right:

- Start slowly.
- Pay attention.
- Savor the moments.
- Push a bit further when you feel it's appropriate.
- Pull back slightly if she does, to the same degree.
- Lather rinse, repeat.

Keep that feline metaphor in mind when approaching a woman you have your eye on. If you rush it, she'll vamoose, hopefully without getting her whiskers in a twist. If a woman turns her back on you, you're not going to get another chance. Now make like catnip and go git 'em, tiger!

Sex, and the attraction between the sexes, does make the world go 'round.

Hugh Hefner

9

SILENT ATTRACTION SIGNALS

You may be thinking that once you learn all the techniques about being your most elegant, savvy, beautiful self is going to be enough to snag some hot dates, and you're partially right. The part I haven't told you about yet is this: Most men will spin their wheels looking around the room for sexy sirens to approach and then wonder why nothing's happening. It's not that they're doing anything wrong. It's that they're putting all their focus on who they want to approach.

Heres' the rub: They're missing out. What do I mean? They're forgetting to notice the ladies that are checking them out! Yes, you heard me right. We're cruising the room just as much as you are.

Once Brad, one of my busy executive clients, learned about this fact from me, he made good use of it. Brad would walk into a social gathering with his newfound flair, and casually lean back on something with confident, open body language. While facing the crowd, his arms uncrossed, a smile on his lips, he'd take a good, long look around.

While noticing the ladies that naturally caught everyone's attention, he'd also observe which of those ladies were looking at him. And that's to whom he would then shift his focus.

He'd flirt with one of those women using eye contact and smiles from across the room, and then slowly start to move in. Making sure she got a good look at him full-length so she could tell he had all or most of his body parts and looked after himself, he'd keep getting closer. Before you knew it, they were joking around together and he'd be working on making his exit with her!

The cool thing was that Brad was by no means the best-looking guy in the room, but he knew how to save himself both time and the disappointment of rejection by approaching an attractive gal who was checking *him* out.

You can have your pick if you focus on the right things. Don't make it an uphill battle for yourself.

I'm going to share a tip with you that may seem counter-intuitive at first blush, yet it makes total sense when you think it through: Spend more time working on the women that notice you. Imagine walking into a party and seeing some interesting-looking women. What's the first thing you do? Check them out and start mustering up the courage to approach? It's what most men do, and oddly, it is the least successful way of getting a date. Why? It's because you have not checked for her Silent Attraction Signals. Doesn't it make sense to notice if she's interested in you making your approaching?

Wouldn't talking to her be so much easier if she already liked the looks of you?

The plot gets thicker. If you're traveling abroad or you're into women from different cultures, make sure you're fully aware of cultural differences. What's acceptable in North America may be highly taboo in other countries. I had a call from a woman who couldn't figure out why her new boyfriend never looked her in the eye. She was also starving in the affection department because he kept such a physical distance between them when they were together.

It turned out that he had immigrated from India as an adult and was not up to speed with North American culture. You see, in India, it's frowned upon to look a woman in the eye, never mind touching her or standing close unless you're married to her. A guy could get into serious trouble if he broke these rules. A woman would face far worse consequences if she were to engage incorrectly with a man to whom she is not betrothed.

I know many men who love Asian women and for a good reason. Asian women are raised to be more docile and accommodating with men. Once married though, their role changes. Be prepared to have her take control of your paycheck and manage both the household and your personal spending. In Asia, it's more important for the men to be cultured than brazen. Alpha male-ism is not a plus. Change your approach to a less boisterous one with Asian beauties.

Interestingly, it's customary for Asian women to tell the man she's interested in him — nothing like in North America. Another difference you'll notice is that the

Chick Magnet

Japanese have a strong aversion to conflict and complaining, even with family in private. If, in response to your question, you get a smile and a "maybe," what they really mean is fuggedaboudit. Bear this in mind when dating Japanese lovelies.

Whatever country you may in, the key here is to change your approach strategy by looking for the women that like you. They may be more interesting than you think. Don't spin cycles on only the ones that catch your eye especially if you get no return signals.

If you've made it over to and have struck up a conversation with the cutie who was giving you the once-over at a bar, and you're both facing forward, take note of these positioning pointers.

This is important because the combination of what you do next could get you a date:

- Wait for her to turn slightly towards you, then follow suit. She moves first.
- If she turns away from you, facing the bar again right after you've said something, you have put her off. Her body language just told you so.
- You must mirror her body language and turn to face the bar yourself, and change the subject of your conversation.
- If she turns toward you again, you have another chance. Use it wisely..

Are you bursting with curiosity about how to take it a step further from here? "This is heating up; I think she likes me. How do I keep it going without it feeling awkward?" Excellent question. I thought you'd never ask. Touch her.

Here are some techniques for different scenarios:

- Take a selfie together. Find a reason first, so you don't creep her out. Make something up if you have to, like "Can you show me how to take selfies."
- At a dance club, after dancing with a cutie, open your arms, look her in the eye, smile and give her a thank-you hug. Makes you look affectionate, breaks the ice, hello oxytocin.
- Offer her your arm when walking down the street.

I know it all sounds complicated but the more you practice, the more awareness and success you will have. Practice this on as many women as you can. Success in life and with women has nothing to do with luck. It's all practice and willingness to learn.

YOUR PUNCH LIST

From now on, when you see female prospects, look for these Silent Attraction Signals that indicate she's interested in you:

- When you catch her eye, if she likes you, she looks down or to the side. Looking up at the ceiling means "move on."

- She starts giggling with her friends when you make eye contact.

- She touches any part of herself, adjusts clothing, plays with her necklace, hair, etc.

- She strokes her glass or straw. I'm serious!

- She smiles back at you. Hello!

- She looks away and then peeks back within 45 seconds.

I know you have a vivid imagination so have some extra fun and start studying how women look at not just you, but other men. Do you notice the attractions signals they're giving? It's even more fun when you observe couples ut on a date and try to guess if she's actually into him.

When you become familiar with the Silent Attraction Signals, approaching and asking women out will begin to feel quite natural. The more you make your own magic, the more you'll see your love life improve!

Most of us have two lives, the life we live and the unlived life within us. Between the two stands Resistance.

Steven Pressfield, The War of Art

10

WHY WOMEN WANT BAD BOYS

"I don't understand why the first date is always the last. Why don't women want a nice guy like me?!" asked Mark, a successful divorced dad. That's a question I hear far too often from single men.

"Women always seem to go for the overconfident, arrogant jerks, the ones that end up treating them like dirt and then cheat on them. All they want is to have sex and then move on to the next woman. It's a game of veni, vidi, vici (I came, I saw, I conquered). They don't care who they hurt. They care about scoring with as many attractive women as possible."

Mark goes on to say, "I just don't get why women are so interested in those players. These same women end up crying on my shoulder when it's over. To top it off, when I ask them on a date, for some reason I get stuck in the Friend Zone and they go find another player!"

"Look I'm a really nice guy, I'm successful, I'm smart, and I wouldn't hurt a woman by using her for sex. I'm respectful, faithful and yet somehow, I'm invisible to them. I'm tired of being lonely and watching all the other guys date the women I want."

Chick Magnet

"The mass of men lead lives of quiet desperation."

—Henry David Thoreau

Been there before? Guess what the single women I meet tell me … "I want to date a nice guy for once. Could someone please tell me where they're all hiding?" Yup, that's the flip side of the coin.

Natalie, a drop-dead gorgeous, bright, successful business owner, and single mom shared her dating disasters with me over a glass of pinot one evening:

"The guys I date are fun at first, but then they turn out to be total jerks. I love going out with confident, great looking men, and we always have such a fantastic time in the beginning. I don't get it.

Last week I was out wine tasting with Pete, a very handsome, popular guy, a CEO I met online. We were having a great time talking when suddenly, in mid-sentence, he stopped, turned his head around like an owl and gawked. His mouth was still open. I followed his stare to the cute brunette who was passing by. His eyeballs had nearly popped out of their sockets, and he didn't even bother to apologize when he finally turned back to me. 'What were we talking about?' was all he said."

"I felt so disheartened; I couldn't get away from him fast enough. I can't believe he did that. I'd spent an hour and a half getting ready for this date, doing my hair, my makeup, trying on outfits and thinking about what a great time we'd have. I want a nice man that I can trust, not a player who gawks at every woman that walks by!"

The surprising truth is that women do want a nice guy to be in love with. What they're not saying is that they also want that man to be strong and self-assured. Of course being nice is an excellent ingredient for a friendship.

The dictionary defines it this way:

nice —pleasing; agreeable; delightful; virtuous; gentle; kind; mild

But the recipe for being good boyfriend or husband is superseded by this key ingredient: confidence:

confidence —certitude; backbone; boldness; élan; grit; fearlessness; authoritativeness

Did Clark Kent and his alter-ego, Superman, just pop into your head? You remember Clark Kent, the nerdy, mild-mannered reporter who had a crush on his colleague, Lois Lane. She wouldn't give him the time of day, yet she had a raging crush on Superman. Same guy, different mindset.

I believe even the most docile person has a touch of superhero hidden deep inside. The Nice Guy has been raised to shelve his inner Superman. It's not "nice" to be unapologetically bold, confident and sexual around women. That's a crying shame. Let your superhero come out to play; every woman loves a confident playmate.

The reason she'll automatically love it goes back hundreds of thousands of years, to when people first walked the earth. It's a built-in basic instinct for women to be attracted to men who can protect and defend them, and their offspring, from giant leaping lizards.

Men, on the other hand, are naturally hardwired to choose attractive, healthy-looking female specimens — good child-bearing stock. It's Mother Nature's way of ensuring that their offspring have the best chance of survival, both socially and reproductively.

A woman's instinct for her survival and that of her offspring has always been front and center in her initial attraction to a man. Things haven't changed much. Drop me in the middle of the Serengeti and guess who I'd want on my arm. Hint: not Clark Kent.

That's why a player's initial approach can often sway a woman towards him. If the first impression he gives is confident, masculine, alpha, emotionally and physically capable and playful she'll be entranced. She'll temporarily overlook the missing "nice" ingredient and a plethora of other red flags. Biologically he may be a good match because it's a safe bet he'll help extend the species. Emotionally… not so much. But she'll have to figure that out in time and deal with the potential heartbreak.

If, on the other hand, he presents as a "yes man," overly accommodating and sweet, but lacking in confidence and masculinity, his romantic overtures will vaporize into thin air.

What women need is a combination of both confident and nice: brave, intelligent, edgy, selfless, honest, compassionate.

But there's one more essential ingredient to this secret attraction sauce: emotional intelligence, or EI. EI is the ability to recognize, process and express one's feelings in a manner that shows empathy. It also means understanding and processing another's feelings and responding in an empathic way, rather than reacting in a knee-jerk fashion.

One of the differences between men and women that can put the Great Wall of China between them is that women are much more comfortable expressing their feelings than men are. A man tends to be more in his head. Perish the thought of "getting in touch with his feelings" — because it'll put him in a vulnerable position. Gasp. Vulnerability is traditionally interpreted as a feminine trait and a sign of weakness.

When a man spends all his time in his head, a.k.a. rationalizing instead of emoting, he is interpreted by women as lacking empathy and untouchable. He's thinking, "I like living in my head. They know me there.

It's safe." So safe that opportunities to meet women walk right on by while he's busy thinking about how to approach them. It perplexes the heck out of the ladies!

Were you ever taught to express your feelings? Probably not, because it invariably led to dreaded awkward, shaky moments. And second-guessing. Being vulnerable, and I don't mean whining or wallowing in self-pity, is one of the greatest strengths a man can have. Believe it or not, seeing a man shed a tear over something that moves him will rapidly propel a woman's respect for and attraction to him from zero to ludicrous.

Easy for me to say? Think again. As a little girl, I was brought up to be tough as nails. Big girls don't cry. I got praise for taking it like a man. I understand how hard it can be to put one's feelings on display.

As a shy and self-conscious teenager, I scared myself into becoming a model because I knew my self-esteem needed help. I hated being a wallflower when secretly I longed to leap forth onto the dance floor of life and show off! Working with a smorgasbord of the most devastatingly handsome male models was like a Cinderella dream-come-true. And I'm talking physically perfect international cover boys. Hello Prince Charming, or so I thought...

On the surface, I was tickled pink to be hanging out with the Adonises of the modeling world. But something was missing. At first, I couldn't put my finger on it because, technically speaking, I should've been on Cloud 11. Beneath the surface, my self-esteem was sinking lower than ever.

I decided to go on a few dates with the regular guys, the ones that were not GQ cover material. Finally, it hit me. You know that saying, "beauty is only skin deep"? Well, it's not just about women; it applies to both sexes. A strong jawline can launch just as many ships as a perfect pair of breasts. I'm not saying that all blindingly handsome men are like this but, when a man (or a woman for that matter) is blessed with extraordinarily good looks, it can be a hindrance.

I noticed that women would flock to the GQ models like lemmings. It was almost as if a switch had flipped. Their eyes would glaze over and… take me… to your… never mind… just take me. Since many of the male models could have their pick, they were not compelled to try all that hard to develop their EI skills. No need, getting sex was a snap!

Certainly, not all attractive men and women are like this. I'm generalizing. The male models I met were all charming, and I loved being seen with them. Their looks and confidence were exciting. But when the thrill wore off, I felt empty inside. I'd not been true to myself.

The big "aha" moment happened when I realized that the attraction was mostly physical. I was expecting there to be a deeper emotional connection, but I had not looked for evidence of that. My mistake was to go into cavewoman mode when life expectancy was so short that survival trumped everything. Having Thor in my cave would have kept me alive, but using those same metrics to evaluate a mate today was not a good plan.

Chick Magnet

I'd been skimming the surface of what could be and never dove beneath it. I got my heart bruised a few times and still... the lesson had not sunk in! I married a charming French model who had a vast circle of friends and an irresistible accent. I thought I had arrived but instead found myself departing with a divorce. It was maddening!

When my self-respect took a trip to Madagascar, I finally understood. Being handsome and socially adept is entirely unrelated to knowing how to have a deep connection with a woman. It goes both ways. I was equally accountable because deep communication skills with men were not my forte either. Double "aha" moment for me. I also kept my true feelings buried deep inside lest they are ridiculed for bubbling to the surface.

You know when you're bursting to be yourself and reveal what's really on your mind to a woman, but you can't go there? You just might get rejected, judged, kicked out of the tribe? It was like that for me.

Deciding to date a different kind of man, the non-Adonis ones who could speak from the heart, was a relief for me. They would treat me with respect. We'd have scintillating conversations, laugh like hyenas and yes, we dove deep into our feelings. That was the real Cloud 11. The best part was that they'd call me the next day to thank me for a lovely time. They'd even plan the next date with me! I had a blast and felt loved and appreciated.

There was one glitch; these guys didn't have much of a clue about how to make a confident first impression on a woman. Their professions didn't require them to do so. It was not that they were unattractive, but the way some of them dressed and the way they carried themselves did not spark sexual attraction. So I'd work my fashion magic and make them over. Even their places got a decor makeover. The guys were delighted, and so was I!

The point is, you don't have to look like Michelangelo's David to attract women. In fact, most evolved women could care less if you have a six-pack. It's how you make her feel that makes her want you. A woman wants to feel loved, protected and secure — with a little dash of adventure, of course!

A word of caution: Revealing your inner self, feelings, opinions, etc. is a bit like touching. It's taking a calculated risk. As much as you want to go all in right away, you can't, and shouldn't. Take it slowly, reveal something, see if she reciprocates, reveal, watch her response. If the reveal is one-sided or laborious, it may not be a match.

If you're a reserved or introverted man, or maybe even a little shy around women, It's not like you have to do a 180° turnaround to be more dateable. You can still be you, only better, once you excavate your true feelings. I love it when a man expresses what's on his mind and in his heart.

"Be yourself; everybody else is already taken."

— Oscar Wilde

Chick Magnet

For many women, it's a big turn on when a guy is intelligent, possesses integrity and has communication skills. Most of the nerdier men I work with are wonderfully talented, smart, sweet and just a few extra steps away from being winners in the dating game. But to some guys, those steps might as well be to the moon. It doesn't have to be that way. With the right measure of effort and willingness, you can effectively tweak the way you show up.

"Action is a great measure of intelligence."

— Napoleon Hill

When you take action to change, the resistance you feel means you're almost home. It's a good sign. Resistance rears its little Gollum head when you want to be different. It's normal to feel safe and comfortable being a certain way, even if that way is unproductive and is keeping you from your dreams.

Resistance is fueled by fear — fear of change, fear of discomfort. It will cripple you if you cave into it. To become that top-drawer version of yourself, first, understand that everything you desire lives on the other side of fear.

You must train yourself to move through fear, to become comfortable being uncomfortable.

That takes courage, and you have it within you. Tap into it. Face your fear, take action. Once you do, life is very different. You've felt the jaw-clenching adrenalin surge you get when you made a bold move to push yourself forward with your career, finances or perhaps sports to achieve a goal. It's is the same thing!

I know how frustrating it is when you've got everything going for you in all other pillars of your life — career success, finances, health, spirituality, peer respect, and yet your love life sucks. I've been there myself. No matter what you do, there's that cursed leap to the moon again. The leap over the ocean of self-doubt and fear. It's a straight shot through your uncharted territory to an extraordinary love life.

There's a big difference between what a woman wants versus what she needs in a mate. It sounds confusing, but it is extremely noteworthy. If you can wrap your head around this notion and take action on it, then as Rudyard Kipling put it, "You'll be a man, my son."

Let me explain. What women want is a man who is confident, successful and strong both physically and in willpower. It's because that man will protect her, defend territory and be a good provider. What women need is for that man also to have integrity, compassion, emotional intelligence and tenderness. Filling those needs will make her feel loved, understood and appreciated.

As explained above, basic survival instinct dictates that women will initially be more attracted to the traits that they want rather than the ones they need to make

the picture complete. And that's why they swoon over the bad boys who eventually end up being heartbreakers.

A gal will go for the bad boys because they show those traits of being strong, confident and well put together. She's seduced by her wants and thinks, "Wow, I have to have him!" And then she's disappointed when she comes up empty-handed in the needs department.

The tipping point to being a keeper is when you can give a woman what she needs — integrity, courage, compassion, intelligence (IQ, both emotional and social) and tenderness, wrapped up in what she wants — confidence, success, physical fitness, and willpower. When you can do this, and you can if you do the work, your dating life will change dramatically.

I know you want to understand better what steps you can take to make that gorgeous woman crave you, so let's get started with one thing you can immediately implement. I've mentioned this before, and it's just that important

Stand up straight and always lead with the heart, it will showcase your strength, women will love it.

Maybe you spend a lot of time slumping at your computer and haven't noticed that you now also stand this way, but women will see it.

One of the many benefits of erect posture over slouching is that you will likely gain an inch or two! If that's not enough to motivate you, you will also appear stronger and more masculine. Even if the gym is foreign territory to you, square your shoulders. That will get her thinking about what it would feel like to be pressed up against you. Bonus: you'll feel more energized. When you give your lungs and vital organs more room you can process more oxygen, you'll feel sharper and more relaxed. What better state of mind to be in when approaching a woman!

YOUR PUNCH LIST

Here's how to walk the post-date communication fine line between being both a nice guy and a bad-ass alpha male:

- Avoid overwhelming your love interests with an overload of affection and texts too early on in the game. Be cool.
- Have a relatively strict set of guidelines, always follow up after a date and say "Thanks, I had a nice time." even if you're not interested.
- After that, at least in the beginning — it should be a one for one. Text her and wait for a reply.
- Understand pace. Not everyone has their phone glued to their forehead; some may take hours to respond. Some may be immediate. Chill.
- Gauge interest on her part.
- Do not over-communicate by bombarding her with texts, pictures, emails, phone calls, etc. You'll appear desperate and needy. You want her to crave you not shake you off.
- After things get rolling, be less concerned about waiting for a reply. You might send a couple of texts in a row if exciting things strike you.
- Always monitor for, and steer clear of desperation in your tone and texts.

Take a deep breath, think proud like Alexander the Great and enjoy — you've just made the first step towards giving her both what she wants and what she needs.

A bachelor's life is no life for a single man.

Samuel Goldwyn

Part 2: Her

11

HER SIDE

The moment Jonathan walked into the club reception area for his first coaching session, my brain went to work. During the three seconds it took to make my way over to greet him, I'd already made a mental checklist of what visual impressions we'd need to work on to make him more appealing to women.

Once settled into a quiet corner we got talking about the many Female Attractor Factor benefits of maintaining a wardrobe. "You know how I decide what to wear in the morning?" chuckled Jonathan. "I pick some clothes up off the floor and put on whatever smells cleanest. Who needs a closet?"

In the same breath, he went on to lament, "I don't understand why women aren't flocking to me like they used to. I'm the nicest guy you'll ever meet." Where do I start …

Was Jonathan an 18-year-old dropout living in his parents' basement? Nope, far from it. Jonathan was a 52-year-old, not very successful real estate agent, on the edge of obese, unshaven, with dirty, ragged fingernails. He'd shown up for our meeting at my business club clad in old jeans, rumpled polo shirt and beat up shoes. He wasn't kidding when he admitted how he made his wardrobe selection. He looked like he'd just punched the clock after a long day at a construction site.

Bar none, every guy I know who shares this dismissive attitude towards his appearance is still single, struggling professionally and wondering why. Johnathan was right in describing himself as "the nicest guy you'll ever meet." He was sweet and kind. The problem was he was shooting himself in the foot by neglecting his appearance. He'd taken a nose dive into the deep laundry basket some men fall into. Peering out from underneath a not-so-fragrant pile of dirty clothing, he was a lonely question mark. Girls were passing him by because he didn't appear to be taking care of himself.

What may have seemed boyishly adorable in a man's teenage years shows up as a reluctance to grow up in later years. He was missing the maturity and experience that comes from having a long-term relationship.

Floating from one short-lived relationship to another, he never got past the honeymoon phase. Instead, he remained a happy-go-lucky college kid at heart. Expecting the same results he got in his younger years without any personal growth and maturity was clearly not working for him.

A grown man can't hide behind the forgiving innocence of youth forever, and still expect to attract and keep a beautiful woman.

A grown man can't hide behind the forgiving innocence of youth forever, and still, expect to attract and keep a beautiful woman.

The truth was that Jonathan's resistance to change had scuttled his present and future chances of getting dates. The fear of the success that a change might herald had him paralyzed, perpetuating his unfulfilled love life. Feeling comfortable with an empty love life can become habit-forming. Even though it no longer serves us, a familiar habit can become both our best friend and our worst enemy. I see this in many men who are beautiful on the inside. It doesn't have to be that way.

We covered first impressions and wardrobe in Chapter 1, but I'm bringing it up again because this time it's straight from her side. Understanding her point of view will make your dating life much more manageable.

When you see a woman walk by, what do you notice first? If she's attractive, your eyes will likely admire her curves, or maybe she has flowing hair and luscious lips. Next, you may wonder what she looks like naked. Do you stop there? Nope, I'll bet your imagination is more than fertile. You might start to wonder what it would be like to have sex with her.

But when a woman notices a guy… Okay, we women have equally vivid sexual fantasies, but the difference is this: We go beyond sex and read things into every detail of the first impression you make. One of the differences between the sexes is that the average guy, as long as he feels comfortable and fuss-free, figures he looks just fine.

Chick Magnet

Want to know exactly what goes on in the female brain when a man like Johnathan enters her line of sight?

Here's her mental checklist and how she'll read it:

She observes:	She thinks:
Shabby shoes —Not occasion-appropriate, out of style, unpolished, beat up shoes can wreck more than an outfit.	I'd feel embarrassed to introduce him to my friends and family.
Wardrobe —Out of style, rumpled, stained, unwashed, missing buttons, ill-maintained.	If he doesn't care about himself, how will he care about me?
Fit of clothes — Ill-fitting clothing, e.g. sleeves too long, pants too short.	He doesn't respect himself enough to pay attention to detail. I don't want a project.
Worn clothing — Frayed collar, cuffs, holes.	He's either unsuccessful or stingy. How will he provide for his family?

Hair - Unstyled, in need of a trim, greasy, smelly?	Scary hair … what furry surprises and odors are lurking inside that outfit?
Fitness Level — Seriously out of shape or overweight?	I'm afraid he'll have no sexual stamina and might crush me in bed! Or maybe his health will fail him early and I'll end up a widow.

It's understandable that, like some women, not all men are born with a sense of style. But guys, it's easy to inform yourself — get some help to find your style. It doesn't matter if you're low on cash. There are ways to dress well even on a tight budget. Ask a female friend with good taste to help you shop at a thrift store. Do whatever it takes. You don't need a ton of clothing — a few good pieces go a long way. If you know your wardrobe needs help and you haven't made an effort to improve it, it leaves her wondering, "Do I want to be with someone who doesn't value himself enough to look his best?" It's a big indication of low self-worth, and you know how much we ladies love a confident man.

While it's my job to analyze how a man could become the first-rate version of himself, all women make split-second assumptions based on the visuals. You may be making your entry at a party, perusing steaks at the supermarket or just walking down the street — our radars are constantly on, starting with what first meets our eyes — the exterior.

Below are some red-flag first impression factors women will notice instantly about men. It goes beyond the wardrobe. Be honest with yourself: if you have one or more of the factors going on, do something about it — unless you like to hear women say "sayonara."

Most of these items are easy to fix and doing so will improve your love life:

- Slovenly
- Dirty (unless you're doing labor or coming/going from a job site)
- Dirty, stained teeth
- Dirty, ragged fingernails or toenails
- Beat-up shoes
- Stained clothing
- Body odor
- Halitosis
- Protruding gut
- Hair growing out of nose and ears
- Leering at women

- Making lewd sexual remarks
- Defensive or offensive body language
- Inappropriate touching

The impression women get when these qualities present is that this person doesn't care a rip about himself or others. He may be mentally unstable, have no friends, potentially dangerous, and has no social intelligence. It's is the kind of man we'll steer clear of.

Men on the "kiss me" end of scale have:

- Self-respect
- Confidence
- Social intelligence & people skills
- A fit body, strong core
- Success
- Style, are well-dressed
- Grace
- Popularity
- Great grooming
- Appropriate behavior

- A welcoming smile
- Intelligence
- Good vocal tone
- Good posture
- Welcoming, confident body language

The "kiss me" guy demonstrates that he has self-discipline and cares about others because he looks after himself. He seems stable, and women feel safe around him. Heck, we'd definitely consider going on a date with him!

No matter where you lie between those two ends of the scale, you are in full control of all of it. Take charge and own it.

Unlike men, we females talk about your appearance amongst ourselves. I'll comment to a gal pal, "That guy could be delicious if he'd just get a haircut and stand up straight." She'll say "Oh yeah, I thought that too. Too bad."

Women notice everything. You won't even know you've been scanned. It's stunning how sharp our powers of observation are.

When we first see you, it's on two different levels — the conscious and the unconscious. Our unconscious will immediately read your overall presence on a much deeper level as soon as you enter our field of vision.

We'll make a snap decision on whether you're someone we should run from or someone with whom we could potentially kick up our heels. This unconscious decision is based almost entirely upon what we initially observe.

If a man meets the "run for your life" criteria, we definitely won't be joining him for a beer because, for starters, he looks like he smells. If he falls in the "kiss me" category, he should start practicing his pucker, because his chances of scoring a date are much better.

There comes a point in a woman's life, usually in her twenties, when she wants more than just a boyfriend here and there for fun. She starts looking for a serious relationship. Men tend to reach that point a bit later, sometimes never. While I do know plenty of men who are looking for a relationship and love, they tend to be emotionally mature and over 35.

To that point I received the following email from a 25-year-old client:

> *"Last night I was at a party with George and Greg, and we got into a deep conversation with a woman about dating. I think she was about 30. She told us that most of her friends would rather have a relationship than a fling. I realized that my friends are still mostly just looking*

for sex. A relationship would be a side effect for them."

It's possible women start looking for a relationship at a younger age than men; after all, we have only so many childbearing years. That ole clock goes tick-tock, tick-tock. The closer we draw to the end of those fertile years, the louder that damn clock gets. I'd give my kingdom for a pair of noise-canceling earbuds. Just like some men, some women are content with a roll in the hay. There are also women who don't want children. Some are single moms or career-oriented; they don't have much time to waste on the wrong guy or a one-night stand.

The thrill of an illicit, wanton fling can be seductive for both sexes. I know a few single gals who prefer having affairs with married men. Why? Because it's safe; there are no strings attached. Usually. Perfect for the woman who fears commitment. Until the married man decides to leave his wife for her, that is… whoops!

Deep down, both sexes want to be loved, cared for and appreciated. It's human nature. Women especially need to feel assured they can trust a potential mate before embarking on a relationship with him. There are many reasons why we need to know you are trustworthy. We may be overly on guard because of unpleasant past experiences with men. Or perhaps we missed all the screaming red flags and got burned because we didn't know what a healthy relationship should look like.

Underneath it all, 95% of women would prefer a steady relationship once they tire of the male smorgasbord. If you want to be the man women will trust and date, get yourself on the "kiss me" side of the scale. The emotionally balanced woman will not want to invest the time to look for the gold in you if you're a walking red flag. It's easier for her to choose the competition if he's already polished up.

When a red-flag guy ask for our number a lot of internal questions are asked. We wonder: "Will he hurt me?"

My friend Rick invited me to his house once to discuss his challenges in attracting a girlfriend. After stepping through the doorway, my first instinct was to run, immediately. The old saggy chairs draped with dusty old bedsheets to keep the dog hairs off, clutter everywhere, half-finished renovation projects and dust sprinkled cobwebs repulsed me.

When I excused myself to use the bathroom, I noticed there was a gaping hole where the doorknob should be. Forget ever entering the bedroom. The whole place shouted: "Get away from me, I'm wallowing in my gore and I'll drag you down with me!" When we did escape for dinner, his truck was even worse — wrappers on the floor, junk on the back seat, fan belt squealing for help.

I know Rick to be a thoughtful, intelligent man in his 50s who owns commercial real estate, but now I know exactly why he's still single.

Now that you know what goes on in her head when she sees you, you have a terrific advantage over the other guys. There's no escaping a woman's scrutiny when you approach. Find out what to do to turn that to your advantage. Use it to draw her in.

You get the picture, reverse engineer your actions based on the desired outcome: Attracting the hottest girl at the party and walking out with her on your arm while all your friends watch in awe.

A special note to the overweight gentleman — pay especially close attention to your grooming, wardrobe, and manners. You must be impeccable to be attractive if you're heavy. Or have a jet. I've heard the ultimate aphrodisiac is jet fuel. Leave no room for doubt about your self-worth and discipline.

Use your new knowledge to make decisions in all parts of your life — not just your dating life — because it demonstrates that you have discipline. All the little things you do with the right intention, all those calculated steps you're now taking, take them one step further. Extend them to how your home looks and smells when you invite someone over. Extend them to how your car looks and smells. The grand sum of it all makes you look and feel desirable, attractive and confident.

YOUR PUNCH LIST

Keep her point of view in your mind when you:

- Decide on what to wear for a date.
- Shop for quality clothing, shoes, underwear, (yes it matters).
- Choose a cologne. Not too strong.
- Visit your hairdresser. Don't skimp; you get what you pay for.
- Are about to toss that double bacon cheeseburger wrapper into the back seat of your car.
- Leave the toilet seat up.
- Thinking of skipping the gym. Think again.
- Wonder if you should invest in a housekeeper

Always check yourself in the mirror before you head out. If you notice something's out of order, fix it. If it takes you more than two minutes, put something else on.

My message to you is this:

You know from previous chapters what needs to be done, use this information to help you decide everything that involves attracting women from this moment on. It's about developing good habits. When it's a habit, whether it's holding a door for a lady, or biting your nails

— you don't have to think about it because you've practiced it so much that it's the new normal. Use that new normal and watch your dating dreams come to life!

There weren't butterflies in my stomach, there were fire breathing dragons.

Emme Rollins, Dear Rockstar

12

HER GOALS

It all starts when his eyes meet mine. My girlfriend Paige and I are lined up at a crowded business event in Las Vegas, waiting for the doors to open. From about twenty feet away, partially hidden behind a group of people, I feel his eyes on me. I've never seen this man before but he sure has my attention now because he's looking at me a touch longer than the usual cursory glance. Feeling a little shy suddenly, I glance away. Then I sneak another peek.

My radar is vibrating and clamoring robotically: "bzzz-bzzz-bzzzzz, you are being checked out, possible security breach." It's like one of those buzzy things you get at a restaurant that goes crazy with red lights and sounds when your table is ready. Why do those blasted things make me jump every time?

The sweet smile playing on his lips makes my heart flutter, and I can't help but look down because he's caught me looking back at him. My mind says "mmm-mm, he's cute. I know that smile is meant for me... what if he sees me blushing!?" There's already a whole conversation going on between us with just our eyes.

Thinking fast now, I hold up my notebook as a shield to hide behind and pretend to check my notes furiously. When I dare to peek up again to get a better look, there he is. "Oh boy, he's looking at me again and much longer this time… I think he likes me!" Now I'm wondering what the rest of him looks like.

This peekaboo game goes on a for a few more minutes until I look up one more time and, "Egads, he's walking towards me, alaaaarm!" Phew, he stops to inspect a signpost in the corridor casually. Thank goodness he is in full frontal view now. I take a good gander at his physique and style. My mind starts to race again. "He looks pretty fit and confident. This guy's well put together. He's even got some style. Wow, this just keeps getting better!"

A squadron of butterflies starts flapping around in my stomach, and I'm feeling both nervous and excited. So naturally I elbow Paige, who's busily chatting away with someone else, and I jerk my head in the voyeur's general direction. I hiss, "Don't look now but see that guy over there with the blue blazer and black hair? He's checking me out. Whaddayathink?"

It's is where our best girlfriends really come in handy. They're like Geiger counters for radioactive men. Paige glances sideways without moving her head to eyeball the object of my attention. She smiles and replies in a low, conspiratorial tone, "He is kinda cute. Uh-oh, he's coming over."

Finally, he saunters over. I feel like a giddy schoolgirl, and my heart beats like I'm running a hundred-yard dash. I have to be vigilant because I'm feeling both vulnerable and scared. The ole radar is hard at work. In fact, I think it's smoking. I've got to look out for the signs of danger before I let my guard down.

While he's on his way over, I use my peripheral vision to discretely take in all the details of his wardrobe, his grooming and the way he carries himself. From the top of his shining black hair to the tip of his polished stylin' shoes, I take it all in.

The man introduces himself to us with a bright smile and holds his head at a slight tilt. As he extends his hand, he says, "Hi, I'm Francis, what's your name?" Then he gives us both a firm, reassuring handshake. He's all there. The butterfly squadron grows. Two squadrons.

"I couldn't help but notice your beautiful scarf. It's so unusual. There must be a story behind that," he continues. His voice is relaxed, low and soothing, yet still hints at excitement and eagerness. His eyes never leave mine while we talk. I feel like we are the only two people in the overcrowded lobby.

A slight waft of Francis's cologne drifts my way, and I like it, just the right amount, nice and fresh. I'd love to lean in closer and sniff the cologne on his warm neck, but it's way too soon. My imagination is so racing away with him.

"Great hands, they feel strong," I think to myself, his self-assured handshake still lingering on my palm. Muscular but not rough, neatly trimmed nails, clean, no hangnails or evidence of nail-biting. I could hold that hand, or it could hold me. For longer than just a handshake.

Chick Magnet

Most of my senses are now activated and furiously scanning away:

- Sight — Style, poise, groomed, confident and… that smile.
- Sound — Oh that voice – low, soothing, well projected.
- Smell — He's clean and wears yummy cologne.
- Touch — Smooth skin, firm handshake.
- Taste — Whoa there, not so fast, Bubba!
- Intuition — Oh, it's busy reading between all the lines.

My internal analysis of the situation is zooming at the speed of light. As my eyes do a split-second up and down scan, I take copious mental notes of all the little details about him. Close up, this time. The long-range scan is already filed away in the mental folder named "Francis."

His shoes are polished and a flattering style. I can tell he has a beautiful physique because he's wearing a pair of fitted jeans, but not too tight. So far so good. I like to get an idea of the goods, but no skin-tight duds, please. A little mystery never hurt anybody.

As I explain to Francis that my scarf was a gift from my grandmother, who lived in Paris, the conversation develops. He asks if I was close to her, did I visit her in

Paris, etc. I love that he's interested in me and able to hold a conversation. By now I'm beginning to feel more special and less like prey.

I can tell he's interested in me because while he's engaging both myself and Paige in conversation, he's now moved a little closer to my side, at a forty-five-degree angle to me. He's even touched my arm a couple of times with the back of his hand to accentuate a point. Once in a while, he leans in a bit closer to say something, and I can feel the warmth of his body. His light cologne is already creating a delicious new sense memory, coupled with those eyes that are twinkling at me.

Would I consider going on a date with this guy? Absolutely! At this point when he touches me, it sends a shiver down my spine, and I want to get closer. But I don't because it's too soon. I know he'll hold back from moving too fast even though I can tell he'd love to. I can tell he's respecting my physical boundaries. Hello, pleasantly exciting body rush! My senses are still searching for something wrong with him. That won't wane until much later, especially if a guy has sex appeal because now I have to do an ego check on him.

There's nothing wrong with loving oneself, but an egotistical or overconfident man is another story. He'll make that Geiger counter go ballistic because he's a menace to my heart. The chances of him being distracted by attention from other females fawning over him will challenge that kind of man's willpower to be faithful to me.

Chick Magnet

Some men are shocked by the amount of detail a woman quickly gathers about a possible suitor. It's merely self-preservation, and you're never off the hook even when we are in a relationship. We may shift into cruise control as we relax into things, but we're still paying attention to the details.

You might be surprised about how much a gal can deduce just by looking at a man's hands. We observe what story they are telling us. It goes beyond the handshake; we've already covered that. I'm talking about in what condition they are.

When Luke, one of my clients, asked me what he should do about his ragged cuticles I suggested he get regular manicures. That was before we got to the subject of feet.

Luke is a successful business owner, widower and a beautiful person. My suggestion to get a mani completely took him by surprise. "Are you serious? I'm not walking into a nail salon. Women will think I'm effeminate or a metro male. Sheesh!"

After explaining to Luke about all the clues a woman picks up and all the assumptions she'll make about you just by observing your hands, he took my suggestion to heart. He's been getting regular mani-pedis for a few years now and has never looked back.

Check out these five things women notice most about your hands, how they evaluate them and how to remedy them:

She observes:	She thinks:	Solution:
Rough, calloused palms	You work with your hands but don't touch me with those mitts lest they scratch my delicate bits.	Get some heavy-duty moisturizing hand lotion and use it 2–3 times/day. Especially at bedtime.
Calloused feet, long, ragged toenails	Yuk! To the nth degree. Put your socks back on and go home.	Gently scrape the rough edge of callouses down in the shower with a pumice stone. Clip, file your toenails weekly
Ragged, overgrown fingernails, hangnails	You don't care enough about your self-image to groom yourself. Or worse, are you even aware of this situation?	Get a manicure-pedicure, learn from the nail salon how to do it yourself.

Nail biting	Are you compulsive? Do you have other addictions you don't have the willpower to overcome?	You must take care of this, it could be interpreted as a sign of emotional problems/ stress overload. If over-the-counter remedies fail, get professional help.
Dirty hands, dirt under fingernails	If you're in the construction or farming industry, great! I love a man who's good with his hands and can fix stuff! But don't touch me.	Soap up a good nailbrush and use it regularly. Wash your hands more frequently.

There is nothing effeminate about a guy stepping into a nail salon for some nail service. I make a point of thanking guys who get their nails done when I see them at the salon to which I go. Mostly their eyes are rolling back into their heads because honestly, it's orgasmic to get your feet done. Polish is optional… Just kidding.

Paying extra attention to your hands tells me you are looking after yourself on many other levels as well. It's is a very reassuring quality in a man because it shows me you have the discipline, willpower, dedication, and ambition to look after me and to provide for our potential family. That's even if kids are not in the picture. I can tell you're a man who knows how to handle things should the going get tough. It also tells me that you're tender and a good caregiver to those who may need it. Yes, my mind goes that fast, slick as a penny through a vending machine. The same thing goes for 99% of the female population.

I've focused this chapter on hands because it's hard to hide them. We notice things in increments about you. From a distance, it will be how you carry yourself and your silhouette. The closer you get, the more details we see, and we automatically start evaluating them.

We check for recently trimmed hair, up-to-par grooming, tidy facial hair, condition, style and fit of wardrobe — you get the idea. Same as you would when checking out women, except for us, it's out of the need to protect ourselves both physically and emotionally. Once you get really close, our attention turns to the more minute details that we can only determine at close range: your breath, body odor or cologne, hair and body cleanliness, loose threads, worn clothing, stains, dental health, misaligned teeth, Sound of your voice, etc.

If we're going to accept an invitation for a date, all of the above criteria matter to us. Bad breath, for instance, is a no-fly zone.

Let's invite the "Bad Boy" back into the picture now. Tattooed bikers are the stereotype, but it's only a stereotype. There are stealthier predators in the mix disguised as nice datable men.

A bad boy can also look exactly like Francis, for instance. Well groomed, stylish, successful, friendly smile. To us, men like him are the less obvious, more dangerous predators. They're harder to smoke out of the woodpile because they're so well disguised. They look just like the decent guys we need to be dating if we want to find a suitable mate.

Within this particular Bad Boy category lies the well-dressed player, the emotionally unavailable man, the commitment-phobic man, the sex addict, the addict of any kind, the narcissist, the egotist, the amateur, the sadist, the psychopath, the cheater, the misogynist, etc.

They may be intensely charming at first, but once they snatch their prey and have their way with it, it's "so long" and "next!" It leaves the unfortunate gal who thought she'd met her Mr. Right wondering what in tarnation just happened. Her mistake was to turn a blind eye to the many red flags and being seduced by the shiny bits.

When they say love is blind, they ain't kidding!

I do want to express that there are also plenty of female counterparts to the well put together Bad Boy and I'm sure you've met a few along the way. Sometimes all a gal wants is a good roll in the hay with some hot stuff. It's great fun, and she can kick him out before dawn without remorse. Hopefully, it's mutual!

But if she's not that kind of girl and develops feelings for you, it's another story. Here's how it'll go for her:

- Girl seeks a long-term monogamous relationship.
- Girl meets a charming, handsome boy and has fun.
- Girl is excited by his attention and flirtations.
- Boy knows she's got her guard down.
- They make whoopee on the first or second date.
- She falls in love because she's given herself to him.
- Boy never calls her again.
- Girl sees him out with another woman a week later.
- Ouch!

Often the reason the above dating situation goes awry is that there's a lack of communication about goals. The girl assumed he wanted a relationship — but she never asked.

The takeaway from this chapter is that after sampling a selection of men, most women will tire of the one-night stands that go nowhere. It's a satisfying temporary fix and sometimes even better than chocolate. But after a while, that chocolate starts to look pretty good. The string of nowhere nights rapidly becomes very vanilla.

YOUR PUNCH LIST

- **Be aware of your dating goals**
  - If your goals are to date around for a while and sample different women, that's absolutely fine! It's the best thing to do after a divorce, when exiting a long-term relationship or when widowed. Rebound relationships are always bound for a cul-de-sac because you're not the same man you were when you entered your last relationship. Avoid making the same mistake twice.
- **Be honest with her *and* with yourself**
  - Be honest with your dates about your dating goals. Take the time to figure out what you want. If you're dating around merely looking for a good time, that's cool, but tell her. If she's looking for a long-term relationship, cool it. If she has kids or wants kids and that's not

your thing, back off because right out of the gate it's not a good match.

- **Take care of the grooming details**
  - Why ruin your chances? Start by checking out your hands and feet. Take care of this business if you want her to desire you. Admit it; there's nothing quite like having the woman you want, desire you. The mutual sexual attraction is like a drug. And that is never truer than at the beginning of a relationship. Trust me; this work is all worth it!

We *want* a confident alpha-man who excites us.
We *need* a man we can count on long-term. We need a man we can have faith in and who has faith in us.

Mama always said life was like a box of chocolates. You never know what you're gonna get.

Forrest Gump

13

LITTLE THINGS ADD UP

Things start off on a good note. Aaron, my online dating prospect is charming on the phone. He sounds intelligent, interesting, cultured, ambitious, and he Googles well. I certainly won't have to carry the conversation with this guy. Phew, what a relief! This date holds promise.

Googled — what?! Yes, expect to be thoroughly researched before she accepts your date invitation. I always check a man's reputation online to gather evidence of social and career success as well as to confirm he is who he claims to be. Oh, and that he doesn't have a criminal record.

The trouble starts when he asks me out for dinner for our first date. Aaron makes the biggest faux-pas of them all. He says "Where do you want to eat?" I feel like I just bit into one of those chocolates with the maraschino cherry inside, my least favorite. "Are you serious?" I think to myself. Steeeerike One.

We're off to a shaky start already, but I give him the benefit of the doubt.

This smart, successful, hard-working, caring single dad has a lot going for him. I put strike one on the back burner and find us a cozy little Italian restaurant.

Admittedly, that little red flag keeps waving at me at the oddest moments whenever I think about our upcoming date. While doing some online research for a blog post, I ask myself, "Why didn't he take the time to ask Mr. Google for some nice restaurant options before he asked me out?" I do online research all the time for a variety of purposes. And Aaron is a tech engineer, after all.

Then I take it a step further and think, "Is he not as excited as I am about our first date? Did he not feel it worthwhile to make the extra effort to display his resourcefulness?"

When inviting your date out to a restaurant, suck it up and do the work, it's your job as the alpha male to find the restaurant. We want and a need a take charge guy. Be sure to ask for dietary parameters up front. Is she vegan, vegetarian, lactose intolerant? You get the idea, that'll help fine-tune your restaurant selection and score some EI points.

Another excellent point-scoring idea is to ask her roughly where she lives or works. If she's driving this will allow you to find a place that's convenient for both of you. You want her to know that that's why you're asking, of course.

Armed with this info, you can now go forth confidently, knowing she'll be satisfied that you've got her best interests in mind. But you're still willing to make the decision.

With all the incredible resources we have at our fingertips, failing to do your due diligence on good date ideas is

inexcusable. It only takes a couple of minutes. It's is your opportunity to impress her with your researching skills.

All week I'm anticipating our date, wondering what I'll wear, how things will unfold, etc. When the day comes, I lay several outfits on my bed and try them on, wanting to look sexy yet not like I'm trying too hard.

A great deal of time goes towards completing my date-prep checklist:

- Nails done
- Hair clean and looking touchable
- Makeup perfect, just the right amount
- Breath fresh, no buzzard breath here
- Teeth brushed
- Showered
- Well-rested
- Shoes shined and maintained
- Matching bra and panties
- Legs shaved
- Outfit appropriate and in good repair

- Pretty accessories
- Light fragrance

All of these little things add up to a shining first impression. And that's precisely the one I want to make, no matter what.

Looking my best for my date is essential to me. I want him to know that I take good care of myself. It matters to me that I look good on his arm not just for him, but also in case we run into any of his friends or colleagues.

Even though it's highly unlikely he'll get to see what I'm wearing underneath that silky dress on our first date; I'll still spend time choosing lingerie, wearing it makes me feel sexy and feminine. I do this because not only am I dressing for him, I'm also dressing for myself.

Wearing lacy, barely-there underpinnings and knowing I'm looking good affects me. In fact, I make it a point to wear beautiful lingerie on a daily basis. When doing this, even if I'm a pair of jeans and tank top, I feel especially confident about myself.

The final safety check in the mirror at the door is the most important. I recommend you take this step too. It's the one where I quickly scan myself top to bottom. I like what I see, and I enter the outside world exuding confidence. Feeling this way is an affirmation of my self-respect, and I know I'll garner more respect from others because I'm feeling on top of my game.

Finally, the moment of truth arrives. Aaron is at my door to pick me up for our dinner date. I start to get into his car and, uh-oh, there's a bunch of stuff on the passenger seat, and he's scrambling to throw it onto the back seat. He knew I'd be sitting there and he didn't prepare for me. Once in, my nostrils are greeted with the aroma of rotting gym attire. I know he's a busy guy, but foresight is essential when you want to impress your date.

Remember that I'm already on alert because of the restaurant finding incident. It's is another warning flag. I'm pushing this one to the back burner as well, to keep the first one company. Now my indicators are flashing yellow, and I'm hoping they trend toward green and not red for the rest of the evening.

Finally, we're seated across from each other at the restaurant. It's a nice, reasonably priced Mediterranean place I've been to before. The waiter arrives, greets us warmly and offers to take our drink order. Here comes another surprise. Aaron barely acknowledges the waiter, doesn't even look him in the eye. Is he arrogant, rude? I'm perplexed. It's is definitely steeeerike two.

When I see someone treating another human being or animal with disrespect, I begin to lose respect for them.

It's natural for me to surmise that he will eventually treat me with the same disrespect when the honeymoon period dissipates. Being friendly with the wait staff not only demonstrates you have Social Intelligence but also helps breaks the ice by starting a conversation.

I'm under-impressed but decide to give Aaron yet another chance. Maybe he's feeling overly nervous or is blind in one eye. We're here now, and I'm hungry. I might as well order something. At least he's good at carrying a conversation so he could still turn things around. He is, however, digging himself a deep hole. He'd better be stellar from here on in or have a big ladder.

Oh boy, he just ordered a cocktail without first asking me what I would like. My hopes are wilting, and my stomach is now growling. Maybe a glass of wine will help drown the red flags. Things pick up as we dine. We talk about his son, he looks me in the eye, and he is a good listener. Feeling a bit more comfortable, I decide to show Aaron some photos on my phone of my handsome nephew. Since my side of the table has a bench seat, he gets up and plops down next to me to better view the photos.

It's all going nicely, and now we're done with the photo show-and-tell. Just as I feel he is beginning to redeem himself, it happens again, a red flag. Even though we're not squinting at a tiny phone screen anymore, he remains planted right next to me, way too close throughout the rest of the dinner. Help, I need some elbow room!

I spend the rest of the dinner feeling uncomfortable because he's encroaching on my personal space. Other than the closed body language I'm now giving him — avoiding all touch, leaning away, avoiding eye contact, how do I say, "You need to go back to your seat now, you're creeping me out," without seeming rude. Plus it's killing my neck to turn towards him in that position. That was a big fat steeeeerike three. Sitting too close for too long on a first date is plain desperate.

Finally, we're finished crunching on our couscous-coated chicken, and the blessed check arrives. The fun ain't over yet because he sees the check and just looks at me. It's a stare-down. The next words out of his mouth are, "Do you want me to pay the bill?" Dear God, now he's really done like dinner. "Yes! Of course, you should, where do you come from?!" I want to shout, but I bite my tongue. Clambering back up to the high road, I smile sweetly and say in the most lady-like tone I can muster, "Oh, that would be lovely, thank you."

I do appreciate that he's picking up the tab but am feeling annoyed that he even asked. We're talking about a successful man in his 40s who's held CEO positions and traveled the world. He should have picked up some dating etiquette by now. Instead, he's indecisive. Are you ready for this? Aaron's struck out.

We step outside, and Aaron kindly offers me a ride home. He's not all bad, but he's in dire need of some dating advice if he wants to catch his dream girl. I politely decline. This date has officially expired for me. I thank him for a lovely dinner, say the food was delicious and tell him I'm taking a cab home. My decision to decline a ride from him is two-fold. I'm processing the evening and, given his unique interpretation of personal space, I'm afraid he'll try to kiss me — in which by now I am definitely not interested.

When I pull out my phone to go online and find a ride, he bids me good-night and takes his leave.

Chick Magnet

This may seem normal at first, but let's look a little deeper:

- It's late at night and dark outside.
- We're in a location that could be dangerous for a woman.
- Who knows how long it will take my ride to arrive?

It was game over. All flags and baseball game aside, leaving me standing there in the dark alone waiting for a cab was not exactly chivalrous. It was the ultimate deal-breaker. Even if I didn't accept a ride home from him, any gentleman worth his salt would at least have offered to wait for my ride with me to ensure I got home safely. It would have indicated to me he was a gentleman and given me the option to decline. It's just not that hard.

I'm left wondering if Aaron lacks in manners, arrogant, ignorant or perhaps just plain awkward. I do know I'm not waiting around to find out because I won't be seeing him again. And I won't be referring him to my single girlfriends.

This date was like that unwelcome cherry-filled chocolate. I wanted to give this man the benefit of the doubt, but things went wrong on so many levels it was beyond hope. Even his grooming and wardrobe were not up to par. He had shown up unshaven and had a ratty, worn-out messenger bag slung over his shoulder

— like a little boy hanging onto his favorite tattered teddy bear.

I swallowed that cherry chocolate fast lest the taste lingers on my tongue too long. It's a pity that a smart guy like Aaron who has excellent potential blew it by not learning some manners and taking better care of himself. Dating him would mean taking on a project, and I don't have time for that. There are a plethora of single men out there who've already done some work on themselves.

Women want a man who will contribute to their life, not suck the life out of it.

If a fella wants to attract a first-class filly, he's got to have the gumption to educate himself on how to make her feel special.

The first date will be very revealing to her. The more effort you put into it, the more she'll let her guard down. If you make little or no effort, you'll probably be disappointed, because she won't reciprocate and put her guard down. You're likely to be rewarded in proportion to the effort you make. Letting her see you step outside your comfort zone is worth it if you want to get a second date.

When one of my first dates admitted that he was feeling nervous, it broke the ice for me because I was nervous too! We ended up having a wonderful time.

Typically when you take a woman out to a restaurant, or anywhere for that matter, there is some role-playing involved. Call me an old-fashioned romantic, but I love watching black-and-white flicks from days of yore, where proper dating etiquette was aplenty. Your date will be playing the leading lady, and she'll expect you, the leading man, to treat her as such.

Next time you go on a date, view it like a mini-relationship or a play if you will. You'll begin to understand your role in this theatre production better.

You're the gentleman, make it your business to:

- Look spiffy (you know how now).
- Pay particular attention to your grooming.
- Do your research on where to take her.
- Whenever you plan to take her, offer three options to choose from, e.g., different restaurants or wine bars or coffee shops.
- Always have backup plans B and C ready. Remember we love a man with a plan.
- Ask your date what her pleasure is before ordering for yourself, then order for her.
- Open doors for her, even the car or cab door.
- Inform yourself about some decent wines that are within your budget.
- Pick up the tab for at least the first few dates.

- Be punctual.
- Respect her personal space.
- Be kind and compassionate toward all beings. Yep, especially the wait staff.
- Keep your conversation on a positive note.
- Clear out the clutter in your car before picking her up. Especially items left behind by other gals, she'll notice them and become wary.

Your leading lady went to great lengths up front to prepare for your date. She did this not just for you but also for herself. Your job is to rally to the cause by looking and being your very best — for both her and your benefit. You'll find that doing this has the same effect on you that it does for her. It will raise your self-esteem to greater heights, ensuring your mindset is a confident, winning one. You'll garner more respect from others because you feel like a somebody. And a really good woman won't accept a second date with just anybody.

YOUR PUNCH LIST

Try to see yourself from your date's perspective — check off these important items on your "before you leave your place" list:

Chick Magnet

- Get a full-length mirror, hang it by your front door.
- Before you check out of your place, check yourself out.
- Inspect yourself:
    - Shoes shined?
    - Facial hair trimmed/shaved, any missed patches?
    - Nose/ear hairs weed-whacked?
    - Any missing buttons?
    - Loose threads?
    - Any stains, signs of wear on clothing?
    - Any wardrobe malfunctions, e.g., pant leg accidentally stuck in sock, shirt tucked into underpants, flying low, socks unmatched?
    - **If whatever's amiss can't be fixed in two minutes, don't ignore it. Put something else on.**
    - Hands/nails looking good?
    - Hair clean and styled?
    - Bits of reuben-on-rye sandwich removed from between your teeth?

    - Breath fresh?

- Before your date, practice mental preparation and visualization like this:
    - Rehearse the date in your mind.
    - Where are you going?
    - What will you talk about? What have you discovered about her that you want to learn more about?
    - What words will you use to create an emotional zip-line with her?
    - How will you touch her?
    - How do you want to present yourself?
    - Feeling less than your best? Give yourself a personal pep talk on the way over to perk up.
    - Remind yourself that you're a good man, charming, witty, etc. by recalling evidence of that.

You get the gist of it. These pointers are not just for dates, by the way. They're for every moment of your public life. Take them seriously. You must consistently dress the part and mentally prepare for it if you want to win people over. Show that you're a conscientious professional and that you mean business.

"But if you try sometimes you might find
You get what you need."

— The Rolling Stones, You Can't Always Get What You Want

Doing your homework on proper dating etiquette and preparation will boost your confidence and your date's level of interest in you. Remember the bit from Chapter 7 about how real confidence, not cockiness, makes a man look tremendously sexy? That's what she both wants and needs.

The world was my oyster, but I used the wrong fork.

Oscar Wilde

14

CHIVALRY IS KING

When the matchmaking agency called Sarah to tell her they had found a perfect match for her, she was thrilled. She had been invited to join the high-end agency without the usual 15K price tag because they were short on blondes. Sarah was to meet the George at an upscale hotel lounge for a glass of wine. George, she was told, was an accomplished international executive looking for his soulmate.

The day of the meeting she went to great lengths to prepare herself, anticipating that "this could be the next big thing!" It's not that she was unhappy being single for a stretch — Sarah was financially and emotionally secure, a career woman. But gosh, it would be wonderful to have the right man with whom to share her life.

Giving herself a quick once-over in the hotel ladies room, she enters the lounge and greets George at the bar. Peering at him over the rim of her dry Miller's two olives martini, Sarah listens to George. And she listens to George. He drones on and on and on about himself: his latest business conquests, stories about his travels, his vacation home in the Caribbean, the one in the south of France, yadda, yadda, yadda, blah, blah, la, la, rah, rah, zzz-zzzz...

Not once does he ask her a question about her. By now she's feeling very disappointed and unappreciated for all the energy she put into preparing for this windbag. Enough already. She decides to take her leave and begins to extricate herself from this incessant stream of verbal diarrhea.

No sooner does she pull out her designer wallet to pay for her martini than George's mouth emits one final flatulence. The coup de grâce: "Thank you for the drink." How's that for a stinker! Sarah conceals her disbelief behind her best poker face, resisting the urge to empty the nearby container of maraschino cherries into his lap. She swiftly decides she'd rather pay for his drink than spend another second with this man.

It would have been one thing if she and George were friends, and he was pulling her leg about the check, fully intending to treat her. But this was not the case. He was dead serious. It's a pity because I'm sure underneath it all George had plenty of potential. Had he known how to show interest in Sarah by asking her questions about herself, she might have accepted a second date with him. He was well dressed and not bad looking.

The moral of the story is, if you see her pull out her wallet on a first date, it's already too late. You've missed the mark.

"Life is a fight for territory and
once you stop fighting for what you want,
what you don't want will automatically take
over."

— Les Brown

In all fairness, sometimes a feller does all the things for a missy he knows are right gentlemanly, and he still gets rebuffed. Disheartening to say the least. But, don't lose heart, persist if you like her. Being consistent with your good manners will pay off. Sometimes sooner than you think. And sometimes you've got to know when to cut and run.

One of my hottest girlfriends, Connie, is an accomplished HR executive in a Silicon Valley tech firm. A stunning, shapely redhead, she'd been through a very unpleasant breakup. (Are there ever any pleasant ones?) At work, there was a certain new gentleman, Rex, a former marine, who insisted on opening the heavy glass entrance door for her at every opportunity.

Each time she'd say, "Thanks, but you don't need to do that, I've got it." For weeks he diligently continued getting the door for her. Until one day he stopped her in mid-rebuff and asked, "You're not used to having someone open doors for you, are you?"

Boom, he hit the nail on the head. Connie's ex had not exactly been the Consummate Gentleman, and she'd endured more than her share of hard knocks with him. It had done three things to her.

She had:

- Lost some of her own self-worth.
- Learned to rely solely on herself to get things done.

- Lost some faith in men, sadly.

Connie spoke to me about the door opener, and I encouraged her to let him be the man. It's his natural role after all. Soon after that she accepted a date from Rex because he showed consistency in his chivalry. They began dating more, and at one point while he was at her place, Connie had some boxes to move. She began to lift the boxes when Rex leaped into action. "I'll get that, where do you want them?"

She was catching on to the notion of accepting help from and trusting men again. So she sat back down on the couch and said "Thanks so much, Honey, they're really heavy. Would you put them on that shelf, please?" Connie could easily have moved them herself. She's a triathlete but appreciated his desire to be there for her.

This story has a happy ending because Rex's persistence paid off. He's now in like Flint. When I last spoke with Connie, they'd gotten engaged. I'm invited to their to the wedding!

The door-opening exercise is not just for men. It's a thoughtful gesture that's never out of place. I practice it, or a version thereof, on a daily basis by:

- Holding the door open for anyone, male or female.
- Letting someone else in line at the grocery store when they only have a couple of items or if they're elderly.

- Letting another car in ahead of me even if I'm in a hurry.

It's my way of being kind to fellow human beings, no matter who they are.

> "The real test of good manners is to be able to put up with bad manners pleasantly."
>
> — Kahlil Gibran

Let's revisit the initial dates where you'll be picking up the tab. One of my clients, Tim, a 39-year-old single dad of two little boys, had started dating again after the end of a ten-year marriage. Tim had a steady job in sales and worked hard to cover alimony and child support and still get to the gym. He looked great!

His views about dating were still at the college level and expected his date to pay her share. Fast forward to now, and he was wondering why the first dates he had with quality women weren't panning out. You guessed it: he hadn't yet adjusted his mindset to the present.

Even though there wasn't a whole lot left after the support payments, he was missing his opportunity to impress his dates with his chivalry. He resented the idea of taking women out to expensive places and then having to pay the tab. I advised him to shift his mindset. There are plenty of fun, affordable places around — take her there. End of story.

If you're not a man of means, do something you can afford. Your date will be more impressed with a less pricey place if you make her feel appreciated and special.

It's the company and how you treat her that matters. She'll feel uncomfortable knowing you are spending beyond your means because you'll look like you are:

- Desperate to impress her and feeling annoyed for doing so.
- Careless with your money.
- Showing off.

A smart, long-term goal-oriented man who "keeps his eye on the donut, not the hole" will understand how important it is to think things through from both her viewpoint and his. I know it's hard to do sometimes when you want results now, especially when you meet with resistance on her end. Ask yourself, "Could it be because she's afraid of moving forward too quickly?" When you note this resistance in her, analyze her reactions to your actions. Understand her point of view and act accordingly.

"Resistance feeds on fear.
Resistance, resist it."

—Steven Pressfield, The War of Art

Realize that she could be feeling somewhat hesitant and fearful of adjusting to the leading-lady role, allowing the gentleman to do things for her. It may be particularly the case after an extended period of independence or an unhappy past relationship. It's is because she's in the process of allowing herself to trust you. She needs time to get accustomed to it.

She may be coming from the "sisters are doing it for themselves" attitude. Now she's in the process of changing her mindset, and therefore her behavior to "we two are one." It's your job to help her adjust more quickly.

Be open to change. When you stop changing you start dying.

Grow into your budding relationship together. Feel out what you're both comfortable with it. Be patient if you want to win her trust and her heart. Make sure you read her cues. We covered the topic about echoing body language in chapter 8. Use that technique here; this is where it keeps paying off. Gentlemen, this applies to the bedroom or kitchen floor as well. Be patient. Pay attention. If what you're doing is working, do more of it. If it's not —Don't be afraid to retreat a little bit. You can move forward again when the time is right.

Also, when it comes to touching, it's pretty clear when she's digging it — she initiates. So, in the beginning, be the instigator with appropriate light touches. You're communicating that you think she's hot and touchable and that you're a toucher. Maybe after dinner, you take her hand or arm if she's reciprocating. You know it's all good when she initiates. She reaches for you. She leans in and invades your space to mess with you. Yum...

To further illustrate how a woman's mind works, let's analyze what was going through Sarah's mind when she wanted to pay her bar tab. To me, it's quite understandable why she'd want to do this. It may not, however, be as straightforward to you. Yet it's an essential insight into a woman's thought process.

It goes like this:

- If she's out with someone on a first date and is not into him, she'd rather cover her own tab, so he doesn't get the wrong message. Most women with integrity will do the same.
- In doing this, she reclaims her power because she's put herself in a vulnerable position by accepting his invitation.
- In no way would she want to feel indebted to this man.
- Nor would she want to leave him thinking he got ripped off.
- She's already given him her time. She doesn't want things to go any further, and now it's merely au revoir.

If you notice that your date is showing signs of interest in you, be extra vigilant in reading her and staying on top of your chivalry. You've learned that being consistent in this way, like Rex was, sends a clear message that you've got her back. Women would much rather date an average looking, confident gentleman who's got her back, and makes her feel great than a Studley Showoff, who scoffs at her feelings and eats with his feet.

Occasionally, you'll come across a gal who scoffs at chivalrous conduct in romantic situations, without even realizing she's doing it. Relax, the onus is not entirely on you. It's a two-way street. If she's damaged goods and unable to play her leading-lady part, you move on. Sometimes people are in need of professional counseling, and hopefully, she'll get some help. That's neither your circus nor your monkeys.

In business situations, a woman need not play the damsel in distress. Entirely the opposite is true. We have to grow a pair and sometimes work twice as hard if the work environment is a male-dominated one to gain respect. It's hard to change roles sometimes. Just like when you come from the office in dominator mode, and you have to switch gears, so you don't unwittingly skewer your date.

My mama taught me to be a man.

She taught me to do so much more than the average woman. Because of her courageous "just do it" attitude,

I can use any power tool, leverage heavy things into place, do construction work and operate a backhoe. I'm physically quite capable, but I've realized that I don't have to be strong all the time when I'm with a date. The lights came on for me when I understood that accepting help from men was equivalent to receiving a gift. It wasn't about him demonstrating he was stronger than me. I've learned that gracefully accepting that gift of help is giving a man the opportunity to be a real man.

Remember George, our windbag friend? Check out the analysis of what went wrong on his end. Instead of treating Sarah like a lady, he made the fatal error of treating her like a business colleague. You don't know what you don't know, but ignorance is never an excuse for poor dating etiquette. Inform yourself more than you think you need to; ask Mr. Google.

A note on those who date millennials: They can throw you a curve ball when it comes to dating and "sexpectations." Millennials like to go splits on the tab, and the women are more likely to ask the guys out. It's is because they're a breed raised in a society where more significant numbers of women hold positions of power than ever before in the workplace. Their predecessors had to work hard to get there, by being aggressive and alpha in male-dominated offices.

A millennial woman wants and expects more control over the dating situation and is often totally fine with having her way with a chap and then sending him off. She doesn't like it much when you ask for her number. She'd instead prefer to you give her yours, so she can call you if she feels like it.

While this may seem like, "hot dog, this is the perfect date!" it can have the effect of making a guy feel a little emaciated in the manhood department. It doesn't follow the laws of nature when it comes to courtship. No matter if you are a millennial, genXYZ, yuppie, hippie, baby boomer, octogenarian or a teenager, in my opinion, on the first few dates you should pay the tab.

YOUR PUNCH LIST

- Pay for date expenses for the first few dates, then play it by ear, e.g., cook for her. It's not about how much you spend. Find fun, wallet-friendly places to take her, like a free outdoor concert or group dance lessons.
- If you've let her pull out her wallet, it's too late.
- Be sure to make the first move to offer help. You are the alpha-man, not her.
- Reach out first when you want to help her, but be aware of how she reacts and make sure she's comfortable with it.
- If she's hesitant to accept it, offer help in small increments. Be persistent, be consistent, in a measured way.

- Don't smother her from the get-go. Gradually start doing sweet little things for her. It'll show her you care.

- When walking on the sidewalk with her, always take the curbside. Before the days of flushing toilets, people would empty their bathroom buckets out the window onto the street. The contents would land right about where the curb is now. Gross but true.

Go out of your way to be nice to people wherever you go.

Politeness and manners are always in good taste. They are a measure of how thoughtful you are, and a woman will notice. Practicing proper etiquette and manners is your opportunity to show you have love in your heart for others, not just yourself. It's incredible how good it makes you feel when others stop to smile and thank you. If they forget to thank you, it's okay, move on.

Chivalry is gracious and forgiving. I invite you to join me on the mission to keep good manners alive — show me the love, Baby!

I turned to him for the first time. He was watching me, not the scenery. "I brought you here because I wanted to see the look on your face when you saw this place." He smiled, and my heart flipped over." It was worth the trip.

Janette Rallison, My Double Life

15

LANDING & EXECUTING THE FIRST DATE

I knew it was a bad idea to say "yes" to this date. I should have listened to that quiet whisper telling me "Esmée, no." My intuition always has my back. My date, Damien, and I are out for a drive, and I have no idea where we are. All I know is it's in the middle of nowhere, and I forgot to leave breadcrumbs. Too far to walk home, no one around, it's pitch black.

I had met Damien when I was out one night with friends. He seemed nice, and I felt a particular attraction. I let him pick me up, and we head over to the lounge at his tennis club for a couple of gin and tonics. "Let's go for a spin," he suggests afterward. "Okay, sure," I shrug.

We're having a pleasant conversation in the car when it occurs to me that I've lost track of our whereabouts. Something's not kosher here. Why would this guy take me to nowhere late at night? My answer comes when he pulls into a deserted parking lot dimly lit by a lonely lamppost.

When I ask him what we're doing here, the conversation turns weird. After about five minutes of this, it becomes chillingly evident that Damien has ill intentions. The look in his eye makes my blood run cold despite the sticky summer heat. I'm going to have to talk my way out of this one. "Take me home, please," I say calmly. He pretends to start the car. "It won't start," he lies.

"Get the hell out of there" my intuition whispers hoarsely. I hope Damien didn't hear that. Calling his bluff I bid him, "Pop the hood; I'll fix it." My auto mechanics skills are limited to oil checking and tire changing, that's it. But he doesn't know that. Hesitantly, Damien pops the hood. I get out, wiggle some wires, and ask him to crank the engine. "Vrrrrmmm-rrrmmmm." A mechanical miracle has occurred. Realizing he's been outwitted, he takes me home in silence. I was lucky and stupid. I should know better than to let my guard down so soon on a first date. Never again.

That was a bad scenario. It happens to countless women, and it's the beginning of our worst nightmare: sexual violation. I've experienced that nightmare, and you'd be shocked to know how many other women have too.

That's why we women automatically look for what's wrong with a man when we first meet him. You may feel afraid to approach us, but we fear for our safety. Sometimes it's a fierce battle between our physical attraction to a man and our intuition. Just like you, when we listen to our libido instead of our intuition, we sometimes end up in quicksand. Luckily, one corked wine won't spoil the whole case for me, nor will it for most women. I love men as much as ever; I'm just more careful now.

I chose to share this date-gone-wrong with you because it illustrates the importance of landing the first date the right way and hopefully getting a second one! It was my mistake to accept the date with Damien in the first place. And now for the good scenario.

A hardware store is a place I never visit without lipgloss. It's full of capable men who know how to fix things. Like an empty Friday night. I'm eyeing a kitchen sink for my place when a guy sidles up to me, "What do you think, single or double sink?" Within five minutes, he Sherlocks me and discovers I love to dance. Here it comes, "I'd love to learn ballroom dancing, but I need someone to go with. Would you like to join me on Monday?" he asks.

It's a beginner class, only an hour long, perfect! Greg is a natural leader, and I already feel protected in his warm, strong arms. He won't let me fall even when I step on his feet. Speaking of arms, he's got some nice biceps, mm-mm! We're giggling, and I can't help but look into his eyes. We're dancing face-to-face, after all. It's exciting, and I'm scared in a good way. We're surrounded by people, and I'm perfectly safe. Is this what's it's like to be swept off your feet?

Afterward, we go for a hot chocolate, and he makes another date with me, for the following weekend. All week I can still feel his arms around me. Aaaah, basking in the oxytocin vapors. I can't wait to see him again.

I love it that Greg thinks on his feet. In the hardware store, it only took him a few minutes to tell me what I needed to know about him. Then he asked questions about me, picked up on what I liked and picked me up!

Had he said, "Can I get your number? I want to take you out," I'd be less than thrilled. I need to know where we're going to ensure it's not some deserted parking lot at midnight in his supposedly broken vehicle. If I'd asked him "where to?" and he'd responded "I dunno, what would you like to do?" guess what my inner response would be: "lots but not with you."

Find out what I like but don't make it obvious. Poke around a bit. If you ask me out with no plan, I'm busy.

Use some initiative. I love it when a man is inventive. Do you find it Herculean to conjure up a place to take the cream puff you just met and hardly know? I can understand that. Especially if that cream puff has a cleavage you want to dive into… Oy! If it were me and I didn't know better, I'd be wracking my brains too. You've got to think fast, ask questions and make a plan.

Here are some first date guidelines you'll find more useful than a pocket in a shirt:

1. Keep the first date short and sweet. Less time to muck it up. Imagine investing in a four-course dinner, and within the first ten minutes, you deduce that it's a bust? You're in for an expensive waste of time. How about taking her for an afternoon dessert and coffee at a cute French café instead? Then you can decide if you want to plan something scintillating for your second date.

2. Choose something playful, preferably during daylight hours. Does she like rides? Forget the Harley, take her to the amusement park late in the afternoon. Sunsets and cotton candy go together well. Oh, how about go-kart racing if she likes to drive fast!

3. Take her somewhere where there are other people around. An indoor skating rink, perhaps? Nobody gets hurt, plenty of witnesses. You want her to feel safe yet excited. An enjoyable yet challenging physical activity will provide just the right combination. She may need you to hold her hand to steady her. You're creating a fun memory together she'll remember. Fondly, hopefully.

4. Find a juiced activity where you might have to touch her to guide her. Excitement or perceived danger sends an injection of adrenaline shooting through a woman's veins. You'll be there to rescue her. Hello Captain America!

5. Be inventive! Boring will under-impress her. Are you paying attention? Good. Now think of the last sweetheart you took out. Knowing what you know now, where would you take her for a first date? If you're considering a big chain coffee shop, think again. Think unique and boutique if she's a coffee lover.

Chick Magnet

Wherever you end up with her, allow me to enrich your knowledge base with this essential tidbit about brain chemistry. (Stop yawning, this is huge!) One word: Norepinephrine.

Say what?! You want to trigger this chemical in her brain because it's the big Kahuna that'll keep her coming back for more. Read on:

> *Norepinephrine: This chemical generates exhilaration and increased energy by giving the body a shot of natural adrenaline. Norepinephrine is also linked to raising memory capacity. Whatever stimulus is experienced in the presence of this chemical is "seared" in the brain. It helps explain how a couple in love can remember the smallest details of their beloved's features.*[6]

The brain and the adrenal glands release norepinephrine as part of the fight or flight response. It means that if you want your lovely to feel a shot of enticement coursing through a woman's veins when she thinks of you, you've got to activate her norepinephrine. When you do so, she'll remember every detail of your encounter in the most delicious, exhilarating way.

Since you haven't gotten to the naked part yet, be creative. Make sure you're close to her, steadying her. Want some ideas? I thought so.

Try these on for size. Take her for:

- Scary rides at the amusement park. You'll be squished up against her in those tiny ride seats, of course.
- Scary movies, you can grab her hand during the screaming parts to "protect" her.
- Salsa or West Coast Swing lessons — couples dancing with contact. Say no more, just look her in the eyes and swing your partner by the arm.
- A concert of a band she loves — music allows people to sit and stand close. When her favorite song comes on, and she's excited, use that carte blanche to join in on it and touch her.
- A trampoline place — oops, did you accidentally bump into her?
- Your turn to think of something.

Keep a list of places you can take her that'll send her norepinephrine through the roof. Customize your first date invitation to her preferences. It is work, but it's worth every bead of sweat. You'll see.

You already know this, but I can't stress it enough. Maybe I should take you to the fright ride at the fair so you'll remember it forever. Have a plan B and C! If she changes her mind at the last minute, be cool with it. Big boys don't whine; they whip out Plan B.

Chick Magnet

Catarina, or Cat, my bewitching Russian friend, was the object of one of my client's desire. I mean he, Marvin, worshipped her. He called me all excited to tell me he'd invited Cat to the opera in the city. Since it was a long drive, he also got a nice hotel room.

The problem was that he'd paid for the three hundred dollars a piece tickets and pricey hotel room before asking her out. He hadn't heard back yet, but he just knew she'd say yes. How could she not? She loved the opera!

Cat called me, not thinking that I might have just finished taking Marvin's call. "Esmée, Marvin invited me to the city to see the opera, and he got a hotel room. I feel terrible because I'm not interested in him that way and he spent all that money!"

Cat liked Marvin as a friend but had made sure to not respond positively to his romantic advances. I ended up having to coach her on how to turn him down gently.

Marvin's mistake was that he didn't read her signals right. He only saw what he wanted to see and jumped the gun. Hoping she would sleep with him when she hadn't even let him kiss her was wishful thinking. He figured she'd go for the show and maybe he'd get lucky later since he was splurging on her. Marvin thought wrong, and it cost him a wad of cash.

Yes, we love a man with a plan because it shows us you're working on wooing us. We want to be wooed. Woo-woo! Um, is there an owl around here? What we also love is when you read our signals right. Otherwise, you could put both of us in a very awkward position, and you'll end up looking desperate like Marvin.

When you ask a woman you've just met the right questions, you'll find out what she likes. With that information, you'll use your resourcefulness to come up with two or three places to take her. She may love dancing but what if she twists her ankle before the date? Options, Mr. Right, options.

YOUR PUNCH LIST

When you go talk to a honey bunny, your goal should be three-part. Think of it as a three-part harmony. It only sounds good when all three voices are singing.

Here are the notes:

6. Gather information on her preferences when you strike up the conversation.

7. Casually give her the low-down on the Fantastic Four things she needs to know about you that we covered in Chapter 5. It's important to have her feel at ease about you.

8. Have two to three options in mind when you ask her the big question "May I take you out to the firing range, parachuting, an acrobatic show…" (Well, those are things I like at least).

Now put on your best baritone voice and go land that date!

Oh, the things you can find if you don't stay behind!

Dr. Seuss

16

INVITE HER OVER

I take a deep breath, exhale and ring the doorbell. It's Saturday night, and it's my first time going to James's place for a date — I'm feeling a tad nervous. It's is a big deal for me. It's only our second date and, while I like him, the jury's still out as to whether I want to continue seeing him after this date.

The moment he opens the door, my eyes, nostrils, ears, and sense of touch will go to work — processing an abundance of data in a flash. All my senses will be working overtime to tell me what I want to know and perhaps the things I don't want to know. Within that flash, I'll have to decide whether it's safe to cross his doorstep, or not.

When James opens the door, my eyes do a quick overall scan. All is well — he's freshly shaved, neatly dressed and sporting fitted jeans, a casual dress shirt, suede lace-ups, big smile. What a relief because weekend stubble, sneakers, sloppy jeans and an old t-shirt would have sent me scampering.

Next, my olfactory glands kick into gear. The scent of vanilla candles and fresh air fills my nostrils. Perfect, James has been preparing for me! It's is very reassuring. So far so good. Much better than the smell of old cabbage rolls, stale air, and rancid sheets. That would be the "see ya later" scenario.

It gets even better when he offers me a big welcoming hug and peck on the cheek because now I can smell his cologne. I love a good hug; it's up there with a good handshake especially when combined with a subtle, refreshing fragrance. His yummy cologne has me saying "Mm-mm, you smell delicious, can I come closer for have another sniff?" I'm lured in, closing my eyes during the welcome hug to take in the warmth of his freshly showered skin. It makes me want to flirt with him! Clean is sexy. Between us, I'll admit that while my eyes were closed visions of a lingering kiss floated by like soap bubbles. An overpowering, cloying cologne would have had me backing off, gasping for fresh air.

James's hair is clean and nicely styled, and when I lean in for that peck on the cheek, even his face smells kissable. Such a nice change from the last guy I went on a date with whose face smelled of the fish he'd had for lunch, yuk.

As he speaks, I notice his fresh breath — phew, no buzzard breath here. Seriously, have you ever been bowled over by a person's breath so foul it could knock a buzzard off a garbage truck? Bit of date wilter, to say the least. I could definitely kiss this guy. But first, I'll need to sniff around some more for signs of danger.

Like a fine French perfume "nose" or seasoned sommelier, a woman's nose will detect the slightest nuances and can reveal volumes about you.

The portion of women's brains that is devoted to scent detection is larger than that of men's.

> *One theory is that women require a greater sense of smell for selecting a suitable mate. In other words, men can mate with many women and have children with each of them and have many offspring in a given time period. In contrast, women can only have one baby in a nine-month time period so it makes sense for them to be more selective about their mate. Male scent may confer key data like testosterone levels (which can be desirable), and information about genetic compatibility or lack thereof via major histocompatibility complex (MHC) genes.*[7]

While you may not be able to tell what your friends have been munching on, I know a gal or two who can quickly detect when you've lunched on filet mignon before seeing her. One of my dates was quite bewildered when I correctly guessed the label and year of Chardonnay he'd been sipping earlier at a business lunch.

As you show your date in, with every intention of seducing her, watch her eyes. She's looking everywhere, isn't she? There's so much going on in that pretty head. Every little thing she notices about your home is making an impression on her, a lasting first impression that may make or break your chances.

Remember how, in a previous chapter, I explained how women are looking for reasons not to like you in the initial stages of dating? It's where your attention to detail preceding her arrival becomes invaluable. Making your love interest feel safe and comfortable will help her relax, allowing romantic desires to stir within her.

It's basic instinct for a woman to be on the lookout for anything suspicious or potentially threatening when entering your lair. Much like a cat cautiously sniffing everything when she enters a new house, she'll be looking for reasons to bolt as she breaches unfamiliar territory. It's your job to help her feel safe, protected and secure — peppered with a dash of excitement, of course. Your attention to this will do much to alleviate her "doorstep doubts."

I always go to the gentleman's place before inviting him to mine. Besides having the opportunity to check out a potential suitor's living conditions safely, I also have the advantage of being able to leave at any time should I feel uncomfortable. It's risky but less so than trying to figure out how to extricate him from my place should things go awry.

How about seducing her with your mind? Keep some strategically placed books out on subjects you're passionate about, e.g., cooking, sailing, astronomy. Make them 'touchable' by having something graceful or soft next to them, e.g., a blanket. Your gal will be looking at your trophies, books, and decor for clues about you and your personality. She's looking for surprises, nasty or otherwise.

A lived-in look is perfectly fine but keep it organized. Books are great conversation starters and will offer her insight into the depth and diversity of your character. Tuck your porn collection away until further notice. She doesn't want to feel part of a fantasy but someone unique and potentially treasured.

When I accept an invitation to a gentleman's home, it comes along with a bit of excitement and anticipation. I get butterflies in my stomach the first few times because I have to like him first even to be willing to go to his place. There's always that initial "unknown" factor playing in my mind. We're about to be alone in a room together, just the two of us.

I'm thinking, "What if...":

- He tries to kiss me too soon.
- His place smells bad.
- He smells bad.
- The bathroom is dirty.
- The decor is frightening.
- The place is a mess.

There has to be some element of trust in him because I'm putting myself in a vulnerable position crossing the doorstep. I know anything is possible, but how will this date play out? There's a slight sense of danger, and I have to feel confident that nothing bad is going to happen. It's a delicate balance between feeling excited and feeling fear. It's up to you, the gentleman, to be keenly aware of what elements could turn her off.

Your mission is to make her feel like she's on the edge of sexual tension, but still in control. That's the place where the sparks start to fly. That's why keeping your home in order is key.

Be mindful of what you say and how you speak of others. Avoid speaking of your exes unless your date asks. In that case always talk positively about them, answer her questions very briefly with as little detail as possible. If you speak of your ex at length, you are figuratively inviting the ex over to join you. Keep your former administrations and hers out of your space by changing the subject ASAP.

Make it a habit of speaking positively of all others for that matter; it's an indication of how you'll talk about her to your friends. You're showing her you're respectful and have integrity.

One night, while over at former boyfriend's house, we were canoodling on his black leather bachelor's couch. In the excitement of the moment, he proclaimed, "I love this couch, if only it could talk!" Immediately my desire for him wilted. Images of him rolling around on the same sofa with other women turned me off. I made a hasty exit. Don't be that guy. People love being made to feel exclusive.

To that end, remove any photos of exes from view if your date is coming to your place. Max, a client I was coaching on confidence with women, asked me to come over to his home to advise him on ways to make his place more date-friendly. At first blush, his place looked kosher, until I spotted a framed photo perched on the coffee table. It was a portrait of a beautiful, raven-haired woman with a sweet, loving look in her eyes. "Is that your sister, Max?" I queried. "Uh, no, that's my ex-wife." He smiled sweetly, oblivious to this blunder.

I strode over to said photo, turned it face down and said, "Max, put that photo far, far away and never take it out again." When you have photos and other evidence of past relationships on display you are telling the dates you invite in, "I'm not ready to date. I'm emotionally unavailable because I'm still not over her!" He was a bit taken aback, but he got the picture. It's okay to display photos of your children, family, friends, etc., but no exes. Ever.

Invest in some fresh-cut flowers for your living room. They're always a big hit. Colorful, inexpensive grocery store flowers will do just fine. Stick them in a handsome vase positioned where they'll be visible for the evening. An especially nice touch is flowers in the bathroom.

Speaking of bathrooms, and you knew this one was coming — clean! This room can be a deal breaker in so many unsuspecting ways. Toilet seat and lid must be down (for the rest of your relationship life). Spotless and fresh-smelling in every corner is paramount. I'm talking about the floor too. Hairs on the floor, especially female hairs are repulsive to us. Your lady friend will probably peek in your medicine cabinet so straighten it up, and tuck toenail fungus creams, viagra and hemorrhoid ointments out of sight. Oh yes, I always look. It tells me everything I need to know.

A must is having a fresh hand towel laid out for her. Don't expect your guest to dry her hands on a still damp crumpled towel hanging limply on the towel rack. She'll wonder if it was previously used to dry your dog and should she sniff it before finding a dry corner? Also, have a fresh, pretty pump soap next to the bathroom sink. An old bar of soap begs the question: "Who touched it last, and what did they leave stuck on it?" These small gestures make a giant difference; they showcase your interest in her comfort.

Let's not forget her delicate ears. Put on some sexy music. Find out what she likes beforehand and start playing it before she arrives. She'll hear one of her favorite songs as you open the door, perfect because it'll make her feel right at home. Don't be surprised if you even end up enjoying a playful dance or two in the living room! Happens all the time — it's a real tension reliever, and you'll both have a good laugh. If you don't have a sound system, get a decent wireless speaker that you can take along into the bedroom should the moment present itself.

YOUR PUNCH LIST

Don't be afraid to let your inner decorator and housekeeper come out to play. They can be your best friend. (We'll let that be our dirty little secret.) Equally important as looking and smelling good yourself is the scent and appearance of your home.

The following pointers are sure to help turn your place into the inviting bachelor pad that'll have her begging for more:

- Barring a blizzard, air your home out thoroughly for at least an hour before your date arrives, especially if you have pets. You may not notice how stale air can sink into the furniture but she will. She will detect your gym bag and dirty laundry three rooms away. Don't take a chance on this one, especially in the bedroom!

- Every room that she might enter should be clean, tidy and fresh-smelling. Don't use those stinky, toxic air fresheners; they are tell-tale. Just air the place out, and try some Nag Champa incense.

- Pay particular attention to your bedroom and your bedding. Should she be feeling amorous, your sheets had better be clean and your bed freshly made. It's one detail you won't want to miss out on!

- Light a few aromatic candles about half an hour before her arrival. Just a few, she may not be into voodoo. Stick with a comforting warm vanilla or nutty scent for now. Works wonders.

- The most significant word here is — clean! The sight of clutter and junk lying around will have her forever unavailable to you. A relatively tidy home tells her that you look after yourself and therefore care about and can look after her as a function of your life and habits. If hunting for dust bunnies and spider webs are not your specialty, hire someone to do the dirty work for you. You'll be glad you did when you see her eyes sparkle. It is worth every penny.

Go to great lengths to keep your breath fresh. Here's how:

- Avoid not just the obvious — onions, garlic, salami, smoking, etc., that day and the day before (it's shocking, the afterlife of the aforementioned items).

- On the day of your date also avoid beer, red wine, sugary foods, sodas, sharp cheeses and other pungent foods. Your breath should have her thinking, "hmm… I wonder what it would be like to kiss him," not "excuse me, I think I forgot something on my stove!" (I've actually said that.)

To a woman, bad breath is the death knell as far as smooching goes.

- Drink plenty of water — about eight glasses a day will help flush toxins that can cause halitosis. Choose water over juices and sugary, flavored drinks to help meet the quota and keep your breath fresh. Caffeinated and alcoholic beverages don't count — sorry, they'll dehydrate you, negating all that water you just chugged. Even diet colas will cause your breath to be uninviting. Breath mints can temporarily mask things when in doubt, but don't leave them in view. Women notice the details. They remember them.

Take heart, the attention to detail you've demonstrated by creating a welcoming, enticing environment for her first date at your place will not go unnoticed. She will appreciate all your hard work more than you know.

Take advantage of the tidbits offered above, and move forward. You'll easily step into being the confident, irresistible gentleman you are. Oh, I think there's someone at the door, sniff, sniff...

Say hey, Good lookin'. Whatcha got cookin'?

Hank Williams, "Hey, Good Lookin'"

17

SEDUCE HER WITH COOKING

It's seven o'clock and, Michael, my sexy Italian date, should be here any minute. We've been out a few times, and to my delight, he's offered to whip up something good for me at my place. What a grand idea! He's preparing the main course, and I'm conjuring dessert.

I've been scurrying about my place, tucking things away he shouldn't see, not until later, anyway. Fragrant candles are burning, and the beat of cool jazz and blues coming from my speakers are creating just the right ambiance. All bright lights are banished. Both I and my casa are squeaky clean, and I'm squirming with anticipation.

Michael arrives, groceries in hand and smiles. "How about some sea bass with organic baby bok choi?" "Yes, yes, oh yes, that is just perfect!" I smile back. Thankfully he'd asked me about my dietary preferences because a filet mignon would not have gotten the same enthusiastic response.

Inquiring what kitchenware he'll need, I quickly pull them out and offer, "I'll be your assistant, anything you need, just say the word." Aside from turning on the oven and setting the table, all he asks is for me to "hang out and enjoy." Michael is in full command of my kitchen. I'm utterly impressed that he has arrived fully equipped. He's even brought his own spices to make sure everything tastes just right. This is serious business! What gets me the most though is the way he makes me feel when he takes over my kitchen. Besides the bathroom, my kitchen is my HQ, and you'd better not mess with it.

Michael shows total respect for having the privilege of reigning over my stainless steel. It's a trust he knows not to take lightly. I feel excited about watching him at ease at the helm, knowing he is mindful of my implements.

The meal he prepares is simple yet sumptuous — succulent herbed Mediterranean sea bass sautéd in olive oil, steamed baby bok choi and mini potatoes oven-roasted with rosemary. Just the smell of the meal in progress has me over the moon — man, do I feel special!

Before starting the food preparation, Michael pulls the cork on a beautiful bottle of California chardonnay, well-paired with the main course. Did I mention I love a man who knows his wines? I'm feeling completely taken care of. What a lovely way to seduce a girl right in her own kitchen! Afterward, bellies fully satiated, we relax on the couch sipping wine, and well, you can fill in the blanks.

The entire event impressed me in a big way, and Michael went up several notches in my regard. Here's a guy who dares to cook me dinner in my house. If it were me, I'd be having kittens. He pulled it off with such confidence. It was a real turn-on for me. To top it off, I was thrilled throughout because of the extra effort he put in to prepare ahead of time. He could just as easily have taken me out for dinner somewhere — this extra touch demonstrated in no uncertain terms that he had taken an interest in me. I felt safe, nurtured and excited at the same time. What made it even better was that I was in my ultimate safe place, the comfort of my own home.

To a woman, there's nothing sexier than having a man seduce her by cooking a romantic meal for her.

It's even better if he demonstrates his culinary skills at her place — now that's a double whammy!

The whole time Michael was in my kitchen I was observing him carefully, asking myself silently:

- How is he preparing the food?
- How will it taste?
- Does he clean up after himself?
- Are his kitchen habits hygienic?
- Is he organized?
- Does he have fun with cooking or does he take himself too seriously and stress out?

- Could I introduce him to my friends/family?

You know how business people will invite potential clients or associates to play a game of golf? They do it because it's a great way to gather insights on how a person runs their life, business, and relationships. Are they a good sport or a sore loser? How do they handle stress? Are they respectful? Do they have integrity? Are they a good leader or team player? Well, my kitchen observation was not much different. And I was delighted with what I saw on the playing field I call my kitchen!

I'm always in awe when I meet a man who's confident in the kitchen because he might be a keeper. There are a whole lot of imperfections a gal can accept under these circumstances. Being the observer in this situation allows me to sit back and check out his kitchen skills. Maybe I could learn a thing or two about how to sauté sea bass or perhaps flip an omelet without it landing on my head.

There are many different ways of making the same thing and have each one just as delectable as the last. But there's one thing that must always be consistent, and that is keeping both the food and the kitchen as spic and span as possible. Montezuma's revenge is never a welcome guest the next day.

Kevin, an admirer, once graciously invited me over for a Middle Eastern dish which entailed cooking an entire chicken in a large pot. The food smelled so delicious I couldn't wait to dig in. At one point he had to remove the chicken from the pan to cut it up when suddenly the slippery little devil took its last flight, right onto the somewhat crusty kitchen floor.

Kevin had a busy little Jack Russel, Bobo, who shed a lot. Kevin did not regularly vacuum his place. "Rats," I thought, "I guess we're off to MacDonald's." But no. To my horror, with his bare hands, Kevin picked the fallen bird up off the floor, disappointing poor Bobo who had rushed over for some serious sniffing and maybe a quick chomp or two. He then plopped the chicken onto the cutting board and proceeded to slice it up for us to eat. Was this his idea of the Five Second Rule? I stuck to the couscous and conjured up a migraine so that I might expeditiously excuse myself.

Another "fright night" occurred when I visited Sergey, a handsome, brawny Russian beau, at his condo for dinner. He'd promised to prepare his specialty, linguini primavera. I was considering promoting him to lover status but wanted to inspect his lair first.

I arrived, armed with a bottle of nice Bordeaux and a big appetite. The pasta was as tasty as promised. Once done dining, I offered to help clean up as there was no dishwasher. "Where do you hide your dish soap, Sergey?" I asked. "Oh, I don't use it" was the response. Seriously? I had to remind my mouth to keep shut as I watched him clean up the dishes by just rinsing them, rubbing off the stuck bits of food with his fingers. Made me wonder about his hygiene habits. That evening I left with a quick "dosvidania" before the anticipated festivities commenced, never to return. Thank heavens Sergey, good Russian that he was, had some chilled vodka on hand. I think it served to exterminate whatever bacteria was lurking on his dinnerware.

Being in the kitchen with a potential mate is a great way for both of you to evaluate if you'll get along should romance develop. If trouble arises at this stage of the game, it indicates that you're not compatible. It's a flaming red flag if you eat off the floor as Kevin did.

If you don't know how to cook, learn. Simple, well-prepared food is always welcome.

Here are three tips this that will make your at-home evenings with her a hit:

- Have two to three signature dishes that you've practiced and prepared at home. Make it easy peasy, lemon squeezy.
- Have two or three signature cocktails up your sleeve that you prepare exceptionally well, become known for them. There are benefits to being "the guy who makes the best lemon drop rum runner slushy."
- Know your wines; any sophisticated lady will be impressed by your knowledge.

So many of the world's best chefs are men. But nobody, and I mean nobody, could cook better than my mama. She was French and taught my siblings and me well. Both of my brothers are wonderful in the kitchen, and their wives love it.

Out of my immediate family members, the one who did not learn to cook from my mama was my papa. Mama cooked for him for sixty years. Sometimes he balked at her culinary creations, like when she served him frog's legs. But whatever it was, she always cooked it just right, with love. She always took care of him. When undergoing chemotherapy, she became so ill she could no longer cook. To his credit, Papa tried to learn to cook so he could care for her, but it was too late.

For the love of Pete, be resourceful and find some recipes that you can master, train yourself. Your dates will admire and appreciate you for it. We all have to be able to take care of each other in good times or bad. It goes both ways. I know some women who can't or won't cook, and I feel for their mates.

Having a man cook a memorable meal for a woman will stir romantic feelings within her. You know the saying: "The best way to a man's heart is through his stomach." Well, if the same goes for women, count me in! Keep in mind that overlooking certain essential details, however, could make the evening a bust.

If you're aiming aim to woo her, remember that 93% of all communication is nonverbal. Whether in her kitchen or yours, it's not what you say but what you do that will help open the door to more romantic overtures. Being prepared when the moment arrives plays a considerable part in helping her relax and feel romantic. That relaxed "I'm in good hands" feeling will set the stage for the evening.

What do I mean by being prepared? Forget last-minute dates, especially if she's a single mom. Arrange the date with her about a week in advance and confirm the day before. A woman will love both the anticipation and the thought that she is on your mind all week. It may not be the case; you could be away at a five-day ice-fishing conference in Tuktoyaktuk for all she knows. The point is that you want to convey that you are busy planning and thinking about her all week because it shows that she is important to you.

Heed your scout's pledge: do not be hastily stuffing a chicken in the oven when she arrives. When you're prepared and know your signature dishes well, you'll exude confidence. Bonus: you'll be better able to focus on flirting and conversing with your date when you're not burrowing in your fridge for parmesan only to find it covered in green fur.

YOUR PUNCH LIST

Here are some practical pointers to help you look like a rock star in your apron:

- Ask about her food preferences ahead of time. Dietary restrictions run aplenty — asking shows you're conscientious. Especially if you're planning to prepare your favorite haggis, blood sausage or, god forbid, tripe. Trust me; you'll want to check with her first. You want to make her giggle, not gag.
- Pick up a lovely wine that pairs well with the dish. It doesn't have to be expensive, don't bring cheap schlock. If you're not sure what to get, go to an adult beverage store and ask an expert. If she's cooking and you don't know what the dish is, a nice bottle of prosecco or champagne will be the perfect icebreaker.
- Have fresh ingredients and keep the recipe simple. This way you'll be able to talk because your mind won't be preoccupied.
- If cooking at her place, make sure you have all the ingredients you'll need OR ask if she has them at her home, e.g., olive oil, vinegar.
- Clean up after yourself so she can feel reassured that you're organized and respectful. If she offers to wash up, doing dishes together can be lots of

fun! Clean the dishes thoroughly — remember Sergey?

- Wipe off counters, pick up any fallen food lest it gets smooshed underfoot. No need to be anal, just do a good job.

All of the above is an excellent opportunity to show your lovely your communication skills, teamwork, and respect for her and her environment. It also showcases the organizational, playful and creative aspects of your personality.

The questions I was asking myself when Michael was searing that succulent sea bass for me are ones any woman would ask herself in that situation. We're not looking to take on another man-project, and there is plenty of fish in the sea. Make it easy for her to choose you.

Every man has a superpower, and they may not know what it is yet because they haven't thought about it. Are you talented with your hands? Good at martial arts moves? Able to leap tall buildings in a single bound? Cooking could be one of those superpowers.

Whatever it is, develop your superpower mad-skills because it'll get you into her heart much faster.

Wanting something is not enough. You must hunger for it. Your motivation must be absolutely compelling in order to overcome the obstacles that will invariably come your way.

Les Brown

18

ASK FOR THE SALE

I just made my solo grand entrance at an elegant house party, and I'm taking it all in, looking for familiar faces and a glass of champagne. Almost immediately a tall, dark and handsome mister sporting a tux makes his way over. "Welcome, I'm Alfredo. Do you know a lot of people here?" He says with a reassuring handshake. It turns out he's Italian, intelligent and available, my kinda guy.

It's not often I'm attracted to a man at first sight, but this one seems so genuine. He's a touch nervous — perhaps my slinky, low-cut little black dress is the culprit? Quite understandable, so I give him plenty of time to pop the question. "Say, I've got two tickets to see a great band, would you like to join me?" Or something tasty like that. Heck, I'd love to go on a date with him! I'm giving him all the "go ahead and ask me out; I promise I won't bite … too hard" signals.

He knows from our conversation that I love music. In fact, I've given him some clues about what activities I like: hiking, wine tasting, dancing, swimming, surfing lessons. Pick a card, any card.

We're having lots of fun chatting, and I can tell he's smitten because he can't take his eyes off of me. His body language is screaming "Hello, let's blow this pop stand and go smooch somewhere romantic."

So far he's revealed all the right facts about himself. He raised his daughter on his own, put her through college in Italy, he has an excellent relationship with her and travels to Italy often to visit her.

From this I've gathered that he has these qualities:

- Empathy and caring
- Discipline and stamina
- Has resources
- Good relationship skills
- Adventuresome

Now would be a perfect time for him to invite me on a date. I've gathered all I need to know and offered all he needs to know for now. We've signaled with our eyes, smile, conversation and body that we like each other. He's already touched me by shaking my hand. What's the holdup?

At this point I'm parched. Alfredo had stopped me while I was hunting for something to wet my whistle. We've been chatting for fifteen minutes, and by now my tongue is hanging out. Will he ever take pity and walk me to the bar? Nope.

Hmm, let's try for the giant buffet. Eyeing the mouthwatering spread of food a mere 15 feet away, I drool, "I've got to eat something, Alfredo, have you checked out the buffet yet?" "Uh, no, I've already eaten." Pfft, that worked well.

Okay, that does it, when I'm hungry, thirsty and my blood sugar dips below freezing that troublesome "hangry" feeling starts to set in. Alfredo wouldn't like me very much in that condition, so I tear myself away to feed the beast. Sigh.

Once sated and socialized, a friend grabs me by the arm and offers "How about a game of pool downstairs, a few of us guys are heading down right now." "Oh yes, please!! That sounds like a blast, will you teach me?" I reply, delighted. I love, love, love to learn fun new games.

"Wait, okay if I invite a friend? I'll be right back." I'd give my Italian gentleman one last chance. I do a quick tour through the packed party but can't find Alfredo. Oh well, too bad.

I traipse downstairs to play pool. We're having a marvelous time, and everyone is doing their utmost to teach me how to play at the same time! It's my shot, and my pool cue is poised when out of the corner of my eye, I see him. Alfredo is coming down the stairs to check out the game. I get the sense he's looking for me because his eyes light up when he spots me. I greet him with a smile and lean in to sink the red ball.

While calculating my angles and getting multiple instructions on how to swing from the shoulder I sneak a peek at Mr. Tuxedo. He's bantering with the other players, but I sense he's feeling a bit awkward. Could be he's feeling outnumbered by the other guys with whom I'm playing.

Then, to my chagrin, he vanishes back upstairs to be swallowed up by the party crowd. There was no "nice shot!" or "Look, your chalice is empty, would you like a top-up?" or "I'm heading out, I'd love to call you sometime?" N-o-t-h-i-n-g.

Once the game is over, I make my way back upstairs to forage for chocolate. Gloria, a petite brunette girlfriend, comes up to me asking excitedly, "Oh my gosh, did that guy find you, the one in the tux?" "Yes, he did find me downstairs. Why?" I reply. "He was asking where you went. I told him to find you and ask you out. Get up the nerve and just go for it!" replies Gloria.

There is a saying in business that you have to ask for the sale. It's the same with women. Ask for the date.

Alfredo didn't muster up the moxie to ask me out, so we both lost out. I gave him all the positive signals he could have wanted to indicate the door was open. Even Gloria was rooting for him! While he was promising at first, Alfredo let his fear of getting rejected get the better of him. I would gladly have gone out with him. All he had to do was ask.

Let me back up a little because Alfredo is not the only interested party at this swank shindig. Shortly after I take my leave from him to head for the grand buffet, another tall tuxedoed gentleman approaches me. "Hi, I'm Jay, what's your name?" He asks. I've already noticed that he's well groomed, well spoken, makes eye contact and is wearing shiny black Italian lace-ups.

We converse for a few minutes while I munch on canapés. Jay's nicely packaged, except for one thing: his voice. It's normal to be nervous in these situations, but this guy is downright jittery. The tension is affecting how the sound waves flow from Jay's mouth. His voice sounds higher pitched than it should for a man who stands 6'3". Either that or his Armani shorts shrank in the wash. I see his jaw clenching as actors do in movie close-ups to look more intense. The whole thing now has me feeling antsy because he sounds abnormally nervous.

The way the whites of his eyes are visible on all four sides of the iris remind me of Charles Manson's bulging eyeballs in his mug shot. It's an expression of either evil or terror, according to the study of physiognomy (the study of facial features). Jeepers, creepers, where'd you get those peepers!

When I come across someone who both sounds scared and has eyes that look like they just caught their ninety-year-old grandma making out with the pool boy, I turn around and walk away. Refer to Chapters 3 and 4 and read the signs, it's over.

Peepers, pool boys and tight shorts aside, Jay seems respectable, but I feel like he could use a little help. I slip him my business card and excuse myself, explaining that I must thank the host.

Here's how anxiety affects certain muscles that make you appear jumpy, and what you can do about it:

Muscles tensed:	What happens:	Solution:
Around vocal chords	Voice raises to higher, more strained pitch	Practice keeping your tongue down and relaxed with the tip close to the back of the bottom teeth.
Lungs and solar plexus	Breathing becomes shallow, voice becomes unsteady. You hold your breath and start talking too fast.	Take three deep breaths as if you were filling a balloon in your abdomen. Exhale really slowly as your abdomen comes back in. Then go talk to her.

Jaw and neck	Jaw clenches visibly, shoulders tighten.	Let your jaw hang slack so your top teeth don't touch your bottom ones. Have your chest up, shoulders back and down. Relax. Breathe deep. SMILE.

Later, while chatting up a friend, I observe Jay doing several more-than-obvious walk-bys as if looking for just the right moment move in. He catches my eye but risks neither a smile nor a wink. I'm starting to feel like a stalked cat and avoid him.

I purposely show no interest in Jay, but somehow he hasn't picked up on my body language emitting a loud "eep–eep, the hatch is now closing." To his credit, he does finally ask for the sale. Before leaving, he comes up to me while I'm joking around with a male friend and abruptly blurts "Could I get your number? I want to get together with you." I politely decline and silently praise him for stepping up to the plate.

Gentlemen, to better your odds of getting a "yes" when you ask a lady out, study her body language and read her signals. Is she opening up to you with her face and body? Or is she turning away and averting her eyes to avoid contact with you? Take another look at Chapter 8 for a refresher on this high-priority topic.

There was a time in my life, long ago, when I felt unworthy of the men I was interested in. So I can relate to the horror of getting a "no." Back then I would have thought "he'll never notice me, I'd better go hang around him and make myself obvious." I would have ditched my friends at the pool table and followed the man who had my interest. No more — my friends are precious to me and so is my hard-earned élan.

That "follow him" technique always backfired anyway because it's unnatural for a woman to chase a man. It made me feel even more unworthy. It made me way too easy to catch.

Nowadays I give a gentleman the opportunity to be the man and show me he has what it takes to ask me out. Of course, I'll excuse some nerves as long as he's picking up on my signals.

When it comes to courting, men and women have different roles, no matter what century it is.

Where Alfredo began to miss the mark, was when he didn't pick up on my "How's the buffet, I'm parched" hints. It would have been easy for him to escort me to the sumptuous buffet and help me select some tidbits.

It would have been a terrific conversation piece and insight on what kind of food I like. If I'd gone for the shrimp, he could have said, "I know a great seafood place by the beach, let's go grab lunch there on the weekend!" Plus he could have showcased his chivalry by helping me fill my plate. I would have lapped it up.

The five goals of your small talk should be:

1. Make her smile and relax.
2. Find out what she likes.
3. Convey you're confident, playful.
4. Show her you're both interested and interesting.
5. Show her you're trustworthy.

Showing curiosity about her is one of the best tools you'll ever have to keep her interested. As I said before, you lead the conversation where you want it to go. Topics will come to you easily now that you know what information you're looking for. Focus intently on finding out what she likes but be discreet about it. Don't make it an interrogation.

When in conversation with a woman, make it about her. It's for two reasons. Pick up the clues and go from there:

1. You'll feel less nervous because your focus is on her, not your discomfort.

2. She'll think that you're the most exciting person in the world, even though the conversation is mostly about her.

Think from the end: You want to go in already feeling joyful and confident so she thinks, "This guy's so happy and interesting, I'd love to get to know him more!" Now you have a reason to ask her questions about her likes and dislikes. Her answers are going to help you formulate endless entertaining dates involving activities she'll enjoy. What you're doing is creating pleasurable, exciting memories for her. Priceless.

Be creative. Who knew your prospect always wanted to try parachuting? Take her to a place where you can safely do indoor parachuting together to get the hang of it. She'll feel so excited and nervous that she'll be clinging to you for dear life. Yes, please.

Most people would never guess that I like to belly dance. It's as simple as asking me the right questions. Be a sleuth and take me to the nearest Moroccan place for a loin-stirring belly dance show and some spicy tabouleh. Maybe I'll bust a move or two. I always liked Sherlock Holmes so let's call this the Sherlock Technique.

It's one thing to go for it and give it your best shot as Gloria suggested to Alfredo, but you have to have the right arrows in your quiver before you shoot your cupid's bow.

Arm yourself with these arrows:

- Ask the right questions, Sherlock. Think on your feet. Listen to her answers and use them to conjure up a date she'll love right on the spot.

- Avoid asking her for her number right off the bat. What's in it for her? She barely knows you. Always, always, first offer to take her on a date about which she'll get excited. Then, once she sees you're paying attention, you ask for her number. Just like in business, you've got to sell the benefits before asking for the sale.

- Practice the Sherlock Technique on women to whom you're not hugely attracted. See how you score. No need to ask them out. You're merely honing your Sherlock skills to a fine point.

- Make it an ongoing practice to research about interesting activities, whether cultural, adventure, nature, culinary, whatever. You'll then quickly be able to come up with something exciting for the two of you to do that you'll both enjoy.

- Practice reading women's body language on women you're not interested in to become well-versed in it. Sharpen your analysis skills and save yourself a whole lot of time on gals who aren't into you. You'll be pleasantly surprised how far reading a few of her basic signals will get you.

While a certain measure of boldness is required, don't attach too much to the outcome at the beginning, like Jay did. He went for the jugular right off the bat, asking for my number. There's a balance between interested and obsessed. It may seem fine from your side and then dissolve into nothing for no apparent reason. Don't let it phase you.

Being bummed does nothing for your self-confidence and discourages putting yourself out there. Focus on being fun and playful, know that you're a good guy. If she's attractive, fun, playful and scintillating, then think about next steps, like asking for her number. The first steps are just exploratory banter to see if it's worth more exploratory banter. And if it's fun, you do more and then ask for her number. But if you're too invested in getting the number or the date, your odds of doing so will diminish, along with your mental health.

There are different theories about how long you should wait before calling that number. Let's keep it simple. Call within two days. Here's why: You're a man of your word, not some schmuck with no integrity or manners who calls whenever he gets around to it.

The other significant detail involves that oxytocin, the miracle cuddle hormone you activated when you touched her on the arm. Remember it only lasts two days for men. For women, it lasts for a whopping two weeks. If you don't call her within those two days, your gumption to pick up your phone and dial may wither, and what good is a withered gumption?

If she doesn't hear from you in a couple of days, she may lose faith in you because you've left her soaking in a pool of oxytocin without a glass of champagne. Hmph. What kind of gentleman would do that!

YOUR PUNCH LIST

By now you've got plenty of detail on her, and you might be wondering, "When, exactly is the right time to ask for her number?" It might be sooner than you think.

Follow this Perfect Timing Technique checklist:

- Make your move sooner than you think you should but not right away. Spending all evening talking with her only in hopes you'll eventually rally the courage to ask her out, will dull the initial impact of your introduction. The longer you wait, the harder it gets, plus, you're keeping her from her friends. The longer you blab on, the more likely you are to mess things up.

- Find out early on if she's eligible, discreetly. Avoid burning a whole night talking only to find out she has a boyfriend or separated yesterday.

- Behave as if you're popular, even if you're not. Introduce yourself to some groups of both guys and gals. You want her to see you talking with other people. It demonstrates you have social intelligence.

- Find out what she likes.

- Check her body language. Is her body opening up to you? Is she making eye contact, smiling at you, facing you?
- Do you get that feeling she's into you, fully engaged? Or is she distracted and looking around for someone to rescue her?
- Touch her gently before you ask for her number. Make that electric physical connection. You know what to do, upper arm, shoulder, middle of the back. Plug into her and get her oxytocin flowing.
- Think of a place to take her she'll enjoy.
- Whammo! Now it's time to ask her. "There's a new dance studio; I'd love to take you to for a salsa class!"
- She accepts you get her number. Ka-ching.
- Call her within two days of meeting and touching her.

To ensure your voice resonates with a rich, relaxed tone rather than a shaky squeak when you talk to the ladies, do this quick meditation before moving in:

- While focusing on your breath, slowly inhale for seven counts right down into your belly. Hold at the top for a few seconds. Then slowly exhale for eight counts with your jaw relaxed and your mouth slightly ajar.

- Repeat this three times.
- Relax your eyelids till they are almost bedroom eyes, keep them that way to appear relaxed. Nothing wrong with the bedroom. It will help prevent the "Charles Manson in the headlights" eyes.
- Practice the above when talking to people in general. See how much more relaxed you feel and notice the difference in the response you get.

I highly suggest doing daily vocal exercises somewhere you'll be undisturbed. The best ones are the ones my vocal coach, Roger Love, taught me. They work! I do them almost daily, and it has greatly helped my career and social life. People take me more seriously now because I sound more self-assured.

Opportunities to be creative abound. It's as easy as being aware, asking the right questions and acting on the answers without hesitation. Avoid being left in some other guy's dust. You've got to make your move when the moment presents itself. Not before, not after.

Every opportunity in your life is as unique as the shape of her delicate ear. If a perfect moment to ask for the sale slips through your phalanges, you'll never see it again so carpe diem, my friend. Get while the getting's hot. Take the chance to change your love life forever!

Money brings you
the women you want;
struggle brings you
the women you need.

Habeeb Akande

19

GOLD DIGGER OR REALIST

"Women are all gold diggers," laments my friend Brendan over his oatmeal and macchiato. "On my second date with Helen, the last one I dated, she wanted to see my financial statement!"

Brendan is a thriving business broker in his late fifties who's tired of being alone. He's got a million friends but not one that he can call his girlfriend.

It's perplexing because he's got an ebullient personality and good looks, and he jogs five miles every morning. Knowing I'm onto something, I aim to solve this conundrum. Brendan's gold digger doldrums are the first words out of his mouth when I ask him about his dating life. Is it possible he has a chip on his shoulder about women because this one gal dug so deep? She hit a sore spot.

I'll never know what Helen's agenda was, but I do understand. It's entirely possible she was well off and was concerned that a future mate might mooch off her. It happens.

From my conversations with single women I've learned this: It's not uncommon for single men to exaggerate their financial status. That may be why Helen asked for proof. This kind of deception goes both ways. Some single women also fib about finances, amongst other things.

The motivation for people to be dishonest in this particular department is because they:

- Have been burned before — my, these grapes are sour.
- Feel unworthy because their bank balance is low — oh, the shame.
- Their alimony payments are bigger than their paychecks — grrrrrrrr.
- Are desperate for sex — powers of reasoning gone bye-bye.

These are all valid obstacles, yet if you let yourself linger on them, they end up being your downfall. A woman will quickly identify that something isn't right, and either walk or start asking questions. Even though I explain all this to Brendan, he firmly holds onto his gold digger theory because of that one incident. It's a pity because he's still single today.

Are these obstacles setting the bait for the kind of women you attract? It's possible because when you focus on something so intently, even if it's something you don't want, you attract more of the same. You actually wish for it with every ounce of attention you give it.

Do any of the obstacles listed above sound familiar? Unfriend them from your thoughts. An observant woman will smell your trepidation a mile away. Set yourself free from this trap if you want to attract a genuine woman.

A very astute "working girl" I once met pointed out the three things that will bring a man to his knees: sex, power and money. Bull's eye.

Agreed, the dating scene is fraught with gold diggers of both sexes. In LA many women have made their fortune in film. Their radar detector is set on G for gigolos or male gold diggers. We all have to be smart about whom we trust. That's why doing your online PI work is so vital.

Most honest women looking for a long-term relationship want a man with a good track record. Not a police record. We want someone we can trust with our hearts, our families, and our finances. Someone who's got our back.

Maybe Helen was a little blunt, but I get it. She didn't have time to waste on the wrong man. And Brendan took offense to her self-preservation. Had he done the paradigm shift, putting himself in her shoes, he might have inquired why she was asking for his financial statement. Maybe she got financially burned in a prior relationship and was on guard too. But he let that question turn into a brick wall.

Desperation and having a "taker" mentality can fuel deception. When this kind of man (or woman) comes across a trusting "giver," he/she sees a golden opportunity.

I learned more about how seriously some women get taken advantage of while waiting at the doctor's office. I had started up a conversation with Roxy, one of the other patients in the waiting room. She told me an unbelievable story about Corinne, her freshly divorced friend. Corinne had gotten a very favorable divorce settlement from her wealthy ex.

Not long after she started dating again, her boyfriend, Joe, started asking her for money. A lot of money. Corinne called Roxy, ecstatic about her new boyfriend. "I'm so in love with him, but he's having some problems. I want to help him! Poor baby has a heart condition; he has to wear an emergency heart monitor around his ankle in case something happens. He said that if it goes off, medical help will automatically arrive. Isn't that great?"

Roxy was onto his tricks in a New York minute. All it took was one call to the police department. It turns out that ankle bracelet was not a heart monitor at all. The device was to alert the police if he got anywhere near a school. You see, Joe was a convicted child sex offender.

The twister is that Corinne is still seeing the loser because… maybe sex brings women to their knees too. Or is it love?

Ultimately women want a man who has built a life for himself or has the potential to do so — someone who can share the load and take care of things, including himself. A man like that will have a career, a social life, tenacity, and ambition.

The man who works hard at his success has a future that won't run out.

Let's imagine two different kinds of men: The first one may not have a fat wallet yet, but he is a professional in whatever he does. He loves to learn, reads books on self-development and attends self-development events. His friends also see their lives as a constant work in progress and productivity. Exceptional people always seem to be around him. Whatever the size of his bank account, he's on the right path with his finances. Let's call him Scott.

The second man never seems to hold a job for long because he's an unmotivated slacker. His problems are always someone else's fault. He prefers to spend his spare time partying with his fellow slackers. He can't figure out why his girlfriends never stick around. He's an amateur in life. We'll call him Bud.

Now imagine Bud one day winning three million dollars in the lottery. He scratches his beer belly in disbelief. Then he heaves himself off the couch, shouts "Whaaaahoooo!!!!!" and goes to the fridge to grab another beer.

Bud splurges on some fancy designer duds and gets himself cleaned up a bit. Next, he goes out and gets the latest, fastest, loudest vehicle. It's shiny red and has a sound system that'll make a city block shake. He buys himself some pretty people he calls friends and throws his money around. His new favorite line is "drinks are on me!" He sleeps in till 1 pm and parties hard until the sun comes up on Santa Monica Blvd. Ain't life grand!

Some women will be initially attracted to the cash and razzle-dazzle. Then they discover that Bud is a slob at heart no matter how rich he is. Unless they're just in it for the money, the ladies will soon lose interest. If they're only in it for the cash, they'll probably end up being bored and finding a lover on the side. Mr. Nouveau Riche can't buy what Scott has built.

Put Scott and Bud together in a room full of women, and I'll bet you my best power drill which one the ladies will choose. Will it be Scott, who has ambition, potential, and a steady income? Or will it be Bud, who has no drive but scads of cash… for now? Oh, hang on, he just left with Ms. Brandy, the one with the overly pumped-up bust and too-short dress. You can take Ms. Brandy home, but you can't take her home to mom. You can see where this is going. Once the money is gone, our gold-digger gal will be left with a broke boor. If she doesn't dump him first.

Money will buy you many things, but it will not buy you a membership to a gentleman's club.

You don't have to be wealthy for that membership, but you do have to be a gentleman. Manners, a healthy attitude, and appropriate behavior are a non-negotiable asset to be able to join that club. These things can be learned, but it takes time and perseverance. I don't think there's a charm school for men, is there? Women will hold men to the same standards as that gentleman's club. Skip the cigar smoke.

In life and love, it's better to be a gentleman who is a real man than an impostor with a bloated bank account.

Women are always evaluating the picture you project to the world. That picture is in 3D. It goes deeper than how much money you have. It's who you are, what you've made of yourself so far and where you're going. Smart men know this.

The reason women prefer a man of at least some means over a varlet is that it shows he's resourceful. Making money and knowing how to manage it wisely is a talent. In caveman terms, he has his act together and can forage for food. His family will be provided for, and he will risk his life to defend them.

At a certain point in a man's life, he should have something to show for himself. Some investments to prove that he has a plan. To a woman, if you're forty and still riding the struggle bus to pay your rent, it's a concern. She needs to know that you've got this.

A while back I was dating an immigration lawyer named Reuben. We had a lot of fun together, and I loved his family. He pursued me, stuck with me and bought me a beautiful but reasonably-priced dive watch at Christmas. I'd mentioned that getting my scuba diving certificate card was on my bucket list. I loved him even more for that gesture because it demonstrated he was paying attention.

For some reason, my best friend's Karla's boyfriend, Norman, took offense to my dating an attorney. One day, Norman referred to me as "your gold digging friend." The reason for his comment remains a mystery to me. You see, at 34, Reuben was deeply in debt because a business partnership went awry, and he lived in a tiny, beat-up apartment to quickly pay off his debt.

Chick Magnet

> "Class is an aura of confidence that is being sure without being cocky. Class has nothing to do with money. Class never runs scared. It is self-discipline and self-knowledge. It's the sure-footedness that comes with having proved you can meet life."
>
> —Ann Landers

When I met Reuben, he was well established in both his business and social communities. To me, that meant he had social intelligence and the respect of his peers. He was indeed not rich, but I knew he was the kind of man that would make it and always provide for and defend his family.

I dated him because he was witty, kind and keen and he worked very hard at being successful. Reuben had a plan, and he had his own business. Passing the Bar exam takes a lot of self-discipline and dedication. I admired that. Does that make me a gold digger or a realist?

They say dress, walk and talk like the boss if you want to get promoted. Why not do the same to attract classy women? If you're going to be the man that women want, study the part and act it. Study and emulate the men you admire, the charismatic, sharp ones that effortlessly attract all the top-notch women. They're not all cash rich, are they? How on earth do they do it? Observe them. If it's working for them, why not let it work for you? Make it easy on yourself and follow suit.

It may be that while you are stepping into your compelling new self, your current friends begin to reject you. That's a good sign because the changes you're making are noticeable! It also means that it's time to change tribes. Or start your own! It's the kind of rejection you should embrace, not fear.

Think of it as being part of a new circle to which you want to belong. Just like any other group or organization, each one has its mini-culture. There will be unspoken rules, dress codes, behaviors, things you say and things you don't. You must behave like you belong if you want this thing to work.

Make it a point to surround yourself with the right people. You are the sum of the five people you with whom spend the most time. Studies show that even your income will eventually coincide with the median income of those five people! Choose wisely.

No one has ever been offended by courtesy.

Unless your name is Aahrrrr Matey, curtail your cuss words. They reflect poorly on you. Your next sweetheart might have a severe aversion to your favorite profanities. People can get quite offended when they hear expletives. It's interpreted as low-class. A wholesome honey-pie will avoid you if you utter improprieties because it'll embarrass her in front of her peers and family. You're playing in higher circles now, show her your best side.

YOUR PUNCH LIST

To attract classy, beautiful women who are not gold diggers, emulate the men you respect.

Start with this:

- Stride confidently — you never know who's watching.
- Stand tall and proud — whether you're 5'6" or 6'5".
- Work hard and smart — be bound for success with every fiber in your body.
- Never complain — take responsibility for yourself; it's a sign of a real leader.
- Take the high road — there's no upside in taking someone else's poor behavior personally.
- If you haven't got anything nice to say about someone, don't say anything — now that's class.
- Lead from a place of service — you get respect when you give it.
- Work hard and smart at improving yourself — curiosity is sexy.
- Surround yourself with the right people — you'll attract the right women.

- Curtail your cuss words — the right woman may pass you by if you don't.
- Do the paradigm shift — you don't have to tell her everything but look at her side of the coin if she asks about your finances..

All of the above cost *nothing* and speak *volumes.*

> "If you have to choose between being kind and being right, choose being kind and you will always be right."
>
> —Dr. Wayne Dyer

Real gold and fool's gold aside, making her aware that you care for and about your family will warm her heart. However, not all of us are blessed with a great family; some families are hornet's nests. If that's you, my heart goes out to you. I've seen the damage done by abusive parents.

Poor family relations or crusty relations with your ex can raise a warning flag. Explain that they are no longer in your life for a good reason. Avoid disparaging them. Your friends are your new family, speak lovingly of them. Assert to her that you have confidence, ambition, emotional maturity and a loving, open heart. Those qualities are worth more than their weight in gold.

The only way to enhance one's power in the world is by increasing one's integrity, understanding, and capacity for compassion.

David R. Hawkins, Power vs. Force

Part 3: The Big Picture

20

THE LEADER

It takes a man with the willpower to do the work to transform his love life. I applaud you for choosing the path to greatness — you're preparing to become the man that women can't take their eyes off. I encourage you to stay this course for the rest of your life. Because once you find your dream woman, remember that no matter how long you've been together, you're still dating her. Stay on your toes!

So far, the advice in this book speaks primarily to single men. But what about women — and men already in a relationship? The next three chapters are for them too — because leveling up one's success and confidence quotient is for everyone.

Have you ever met someone who has a certain *je ne sais quoi* that makes you want to be in their presence? People naturally flock to them because they seem to light up the room when they enter it. "What is it about them?" It's a unique combination of charm, presentation, and leadership.

You may be thinking "But aren't all leaders natural born? You can't just learn that, can you?" Think again.

Chick Magnet

We're all born with the same genius and consciousness; it's what you do with it that makes you who you are. You've already learned how to be charming, resourceful, confident and well dressed in this book. You're almost home! You can learn how to become a leader, but not just any kind of leader.

Let's talk about the kind of leadership that'll make you magnetic —like that person everyone wants to be around. Usually, they are service-based leaders. That means they lead with passion, humility, and heart; they take the initiative to be of service to others. They don't expect anything in return, and they don't boast. They're the kind of people with whom you should surround yourself.

> "The way to become that exciting person whom people want to know is straightforward. We merely picture the kind of person we want to be and surrender all the negative feelings and blocks that prevent us from being that. What happens, then, is that all we need to have and to do will automatically fall into place. This is because, in contrast to having and doing, the level of being has the most power and energy. When given priority, it automatically integrates and organizes one's activities. This mechanism is evidenced in the common experience, "What we hold in mind tends to manifest."
>
> — David R. Hawkins, Letting Go: The Pathway of Surrender

By emulating this kind of leadership, others will want to be around you. You'll achieve more success in your life because you're helping others. You're doing your absolute best and then some, every single day. This is how you'll attract more business, more love, and more like-minded people. In the end, it's all about building relationships and trust with others.

The kind of leadership I'm talking about isn't about politics or being the head of a large corporation. It's not about force; it's about power. It's confident leadership that comes from a place of serving others. It means that instead of stepping over a piece of trash on the street, you pick it up and put it in the trash can, without complaining or telling anyone about it. It's not done to aggrandize yourself; it's done for the greater good. It's a daily practice. Simple.

Stepping up to the plate to be this kind of leader can start a domino effect because others will take your example and run with it. You're setting a brave new standard for them. Are you choosing to be this kind of leader? The world needs you because no one else is coming. They're all on the sidelines shuffling their feet. It's up to us to take the initiative.

I've experienced many different cultures and social classes. There isn't a place in the world where honestly striving to be the best version of oneself and helping others is frowned upon. It's universal.

If you want to create a better life for yourself, then it's your job to attract higher quality people into your circle. You do that by recognizing and practicing the right kind of leadership. When you go the extra mile, others follow. Remember those five people we talked about in Chapter 19 of which you are the sum? Those are the ones you want to associate with. Make that non-negotiable for yourself.

The valuable information in the remaining chapters of this book is all-encompassing. Use it to your advantage and make yourself magnetic to the right people. The quickest way to gain more confidence in yourself and be a leader is to imbue confidence in those around you through words of encouragement, words of appreciation and heartfelt nonjudgmental guidance.

Hold yourself and them to a higher standard. Being confident and building confidence in others is synonymous. Can you separate the two? I don't think so. It's like the theory about waves and particles. It just depends on which millisecond you happen to be looking at them.

Here are three key points to consider in life, love, and business. They'll make you the kind of leader others seek out and follow.

Ask yourself:

1. **What are the main requirements I should have?**

   Let's, for the sake of argument, imagine that you are a used car. You're being presented to a potential customer for purchase. That customer happens to be someone you want in your circle. Now let's say that you have the basic requirements to be driven off the lot: doors, wheels, windows, an engine, brakes, gas pedal, seats, ventilation, etc.

But what does your customer notice?:

- Older car (not in a vintage way)
- Nearly bald tires
- Old-school roll-up windows
- Gas-guzzling V8 engine
- No A/C
- Malodorous stain-encrusted vinyl seats
- Grimy steering wheel
- Greasy fast food wrappers on the floor
- Dripping oil pan

Sure, you could drive it off the lot. But would that be enough to entice a discerning customer to buy that car?

Nope, they're afraid to get in. "What if the engine blows up? It smells like a wet dog in here" they're thinking. And, God forbid, what if one of their friends saw them driving this heap around town! They'd have to put a paper bag on their head with holes poked in for the eyes.

The only way they'd buy that jalopy is if they were a mechanic who had time for a project. They'd undervalue it and lowball their offer because of all the work it'd take to make this beater presentable.

I experienced just such a vehicle when my ride picked me up at the airport on a visit to St. Petersburg, Russia. The windshield was cracked straight across, the roll-up windows were jammed shut, and the seat belt was broken along with the A/C and fan. It was the height of a humid summer; it felt like 180°F in the car. Plus the driver smelled like a billy goat. Infernal. I wanted to kick out the windshield and hurl myself out.

The basic requirements are essential for the vehicle to work, but your customer is going to turn on their heel and gallop off toward something more appetizing.

2. What would exceed someone's expectation of me?

Okay, let's take it to the next level. Let's say you were a nice car, one that would exceed the customer's expectation. What would that look like?

Well of course you'd have:

- Power windows and doors
- A/C
- Leather seats
- Audio system

- CD player
- Sunroof
- Keyless entry and starter
- High-end tires
- Navigation system

If you were that car, what would you be like? Remember now; the customer is a discerning one you want to be around. They take good care of themselves and are well-respected. They've got an eye-catching style and an easy way about them.

You want to get their attention, don't you? "Honk-honk, buy me!" If you were the nicer car you'd always be gracious and helpful. You'd always show up to work, or anywhere for that matter, appropriately dressed. Your hair would be neatly styled and your nails in good shape.

Your posture would be good; you'd lead with a confident smile. Your wardrobe would be up-to-date and fit well. You'd look like you take care of yourself by eating well and working out regularly. Now it gets a little more interesting. The customer is looking you over.

Whether they're cruising to buy a car or looking to engage in conversation with you, this level would exceed someone's expectations.

3. How could I be a person's "delighter"?

Now let's imagine a top-of-the-line, latest model car with an elegant silhouette. It's beautifully appointed, luxurious but not too flashy, something that most people would lust after.

What might that look like?:

- Soft leather seats with built-in A/C (love that!)
- Car party-style sound system
- Ping-pong table sized, voice-activated display panel
- Road-hugging tires and suspension
- Around-the-corner-seeing headlights
- Elegant design
- Long-range electric engine
- Internet connectivity
- Expletive-worthy acceleration

"Wow, let's take that baby for a spin!" your customer's thinking. They take a step back to admire the car's sleek lines. Then they slide onto the leather driver's seat, take a deep inhale and get a whiff of that new car smell. They stroke the suede dashboard and wrap their hands firmly yet lovingly around the steering wheel.

They turn on the audio system and start moving the music, "Oh, these speakers make me feel like dancing!" A grin is appearing on their face, they play with all the pretty buttons, wondering which one is the eject button. This car is so James Bond and solid, your customer feels completely safe and protected. Oh, and excited about taking it for a spin. "How fast does this go?" The seat hugs their body contours like a good lover. They sure weren't expecting that!

They're already anticipating the rush once they step on the accelerator. This ride is going home with me, baby. They can't help but smile, and fall in love with it!

How would that translate that into you, the merchandise? That's how I want you to think about your presence, in everything that you do. A "delighter" presence is a gift you give of yourself to others. When you genuinely share a positive, helpful attitude with an open heart, people can't help but want to bask in your light.

This chapter isn't about being a flashy new luxury car. It's about who you are and how you carry yourself in your life. After all, a person could easily have a few miles on them and still be a delighter as long as they put in the extra effort.

YOUR PUNCH LIST

Now that you know what a leader is, here's how to get there. Practice the exercises below on a daily basis and watch the magic of *je ne sais quoi* draw all the right people to you:

- Go above and beyond the call of duty in everything you do.
- Do it with a smile, be a service-based leader.
- Practice random acts of kindness.
- Don't tell others that you did it.
- Act with integrity and empathy in every little thing you do.
- Have a kind word of affirmation for everyone — the boss, the person in the wheelchair, the person you hate.
- Show respect for yourself and others by taking superb care of yourself.
- Take the initiative even when the task is unpleasant.
- Do the unexpected for others.
- Be a giver, not a taker.
- Work hard and smart.

- Be respectful.
- When you fall down, get back up.
- Take responsibility for yourself, don't blame your misgivings on others.
- Surround yourself with exceptional people.
- Remember that no one is better than you, and you're not better than anyone else.

Your leader's attitude will attract like-minded people. Be what you want to attract. Voilà, the keys to the kingdom of Magnetic Presence are now officially yours. Pass it on.

Good manners will open doors that the best education cannot.

Clarence Thomas

21

GOOD MANNERS

When I was growing up, putting my elbows on the table at dinner was a cardinal sin. As punishment, my papa would come over from the head of the table, grab my forearm and bang my elbow hard three times on the thick wooden dining table. I can still hear the dinner plates and silver rattling. My siblings would stop talking, and my dad would chuckle.

My parents were both European, with Spartan ways, and that's how I had my table manners drilled into me as a kid in Holland. At the time I felt humiliated and angry. Talking back was a bad idea, so I kept my mouth shut. It didn't seem fair, but those manners are forever embedded in my memory.

I forgave my papa long ago. He had a strict upbringing as an aristocrat in the Netherlands during the WWII German occupation. I know they had a rough time of it. From the stories they told us, back then the punishment for bad manners was substantially more severe than what was doled out to my siblings and me. We had it easy! Curiously, at home, his table manners were somewhat less than perfect because, well, he had a rebellious streak. But papa made sure we learned them because he knew their value all too well.

Chick Magnet

My mama had eyes in the back of her head — and on the sides — she could spot a dining faux-pas from a hundred yards. One wrong move and she'd vociferate loudly *"pas de coudes sur la table!"* (no elbows on the table!). She grew up in Paris during the German occupation, and her manners were drilled into her by the austere nuns at the convent where she went to school. She knew every nuance — even passing the salt the wrong way was cause for reprimand. The French are notoriously picky about politesse.

Things are different now, especially in North America. Too lax, in my opinion, are these habits:

- Kids leave the table before everyone else is done. It is is disrespectful to the parents.
- Families gobble in silence, eyes glued to the TV. Dinner is often the only time of day families are gathered. It's a time for togetherness and communication, not paying homage to the idiot box.
- Couples and families take phone calls, text and post on social media when dining together. The kids are given electronics to play with during dinner. Look around you next time you eat out. It's incredibly rude. Stay home if you can't spend a couple of hours without your electrotech fix.

Just like it's smart to dress a notch above, it's equally wise to mind your P's and Q's at the dining table. It's even more important if you're attending an event where the public eye will be on you. Not to mention when you're on a date.

If your manners are sloppy, you may not be aware, but others will notice. And you never know who's going to be your next big client or a hot date. This is one department where ignorance is no excuse, because to others, you could appear conspicuously uncultured. To some, you may even give the impression you're unsavory and get crossed off their list. It's a big turnoff, and by then it's too late to right the ship.

Practicing good manners is essential to show you have respect, not only for yourself but also for others. That goes for both sexes. Plenty of women also pick their teeth at the table. Simply put, poor etiquette makes others feel uncomfortable.

There's a word in French that describes an uncultured person — *"insortable."* Roughly translated: "you can dress someone up, but you can't take them out." It would be a pity to get passed over for a sweet job offer because you unwittingly used the backhanded "caveman fork clutch" to spear your food. L'Horreur! People don't want to embarrass you by pointing your foible out to you if they're unfamiliar with you. They'll just choose not to do business with you or date you.

"Good manners sometimes means simply putting up with other people's bad manners."

—H. Jackson Brown, Jr.

Curtis, a man I dated a few times, was one of the sweetest, most compassionate men you'll ever meet. We had a lot of fun together, but there was one quirk that always got me. When eating, he would rest his forearm on the table, right between the edge of the table and his plate. He'd then lean over his plate on his arm, shoulders hunched, almost as if he didn't have the strength to hold himself up. He'd plant the other elbow on the table and shovel food into his mouth using the planted elbow as a cantilever.

You'd think this mannerism would be unique to truckers hovering over a mess of corned beef hash. Wrong, I observe it some of the finest restaurants. Eventually, I stopped seeing Curtis because his resistance to cultural finesse was off-putting. It signaled to me that, as a grown man, he wasn't about to leave his disdain for social proprieties behind. It made me wonder if he ever clipped his toenails. Yes, a woman's brain goes in that direction.

Most refined gentlemen would be uncomfortable introducing a woman short on social graces to his peers or his family — no matter how beautiful she is. I would not have felt at ease inviting Curtis to dinner at my parents' house, nor out to lunch with my friends. Who knows what other dining oddities he has up his sleeve. Perhaps a booming belch or two?

Learning manners the way I did wasn't much fun for me, but I'm thankful for them now. I can attend any upscale event and feel right at home both at the table and in socializing. It's been the norm for me since I was a little girl. It may seem old school, but the truth is, good manners never go out of style.

As explained in Chapter 20, go the extra mile, improve yourself continually. Others will feel more comfortable around you and follow your lead. Set the example you'd want your kids or younger relatives to follow. Wouldn't you want them to have access to the best quality people and places in their lives? Why not start with yourself?

Chick Magnet

If you travel abroad, having proper table manner is non-negotiable. People will hesitate to invite you a second time if you eat like a caveman, don't know how to correctly pass the pepper or are stumped about which fork to use. You'll have made them lose face.

My impeccably mannered dentist, Ray, is always good for a giggle. Last time he had me laughing so hard I nearly choked on the barrel-sized chunk of cotton he'd jammed inside my cheek! He was telling me about a chi-chi gala event he attended in Europe.

Ray explained how he was seated at the table chatting with the other guests. The dining table was expertly set, complete with an array of plates, artillery of cutlery, water goblets, champagne flutes and wine glasses. Spotless linens, spotless waiters, the whole schlemiel. The Veuve Cliquot was poured and the host raised his glass to utter a toast. "Blah, blah, blah, everyone, please raise your glass, etc." When Ray reached over to his right for his glass of bubbly, it was half empty.

Puzzled, he looked at over at his neighbor to the right who was now reaching for what he thought was his glass. In that pregnant silence when all the guests were poised, glass in hand, just as the host opened his mouth to make his toast, Ray cried out in disbelief, "Did you just drink out of my glass?!" The entire room full of people turned around and glared at him for his untimely utterance.

It can be baffling when you're out somewhere elegant, and you're faced with a glut of unfamiliar goblets and bread plates. What to do? I was blessed to have the upbringing I had. My siblings and I took turns setting the table every night, so tableware placement is second nature to me. Not everyone is so lucky — they probably have nicer elbows too.

Here's a great rule of thumb to remember where your glass is when you're parched: BMW, or Bread, Meal, Water, in that order. The Bread is on your left, the Meal is in the middle and the Water (and other beverages) are on the right. It's that easy!

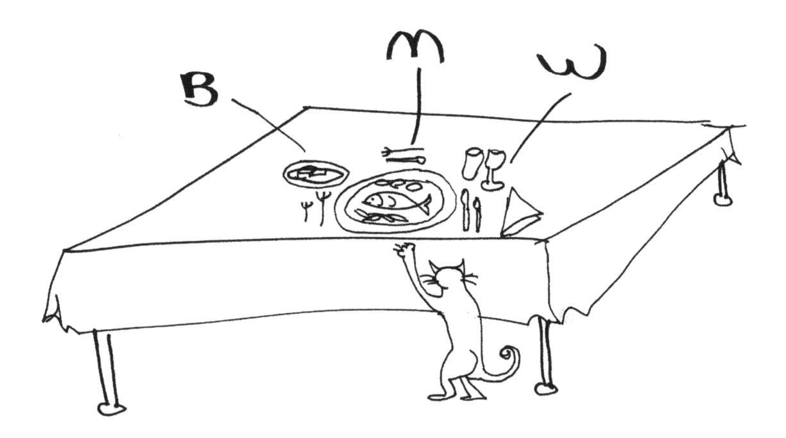

With the cutlery it's even easier; start from the outside and work your way in. The salad or appetizer is traditionally served first, so use the fork and knife on the outside and so forth. The dessert spoon and fork is placed at the top of the plate, so hold off on touching those until the sweet stuff arrives.

A certain level of politesse, not just table manners, is critical in social settings. It's like the rules of a game. When everyone respects the rules of etiquette, you can carry on with your business unhindered. You can rest assured that the person next to you is not going to eat with their mouth open and make disgusting sounds. Or worse, talk with food in their mouth.

Whenever I see a wad of half-mashed food rolling around on someone's tongue like a ruminating cow chewing on a cud while they tell a story, I have to stop myself from saying, "Swallow the darn thing before you speak. It's worth the wait, trust me"; it's so distracting. I'd be too preoccupied thinking "Holy cow, what if some of that cud accidentally gets ejected and lands on my plate while you're clucking on!"

Sometimes we're taken by surprise and don't know what's proper. Depending on the culture, do you nibble on the frog's leg with your fingers or use your fork and knife? In that case, be cool. Rather than asking someone, skip a beat before digging in. When in Rome... Observe what others are doing and follow their example.

The golden rule is to think of what you can do for others.

It could be a small thing like when you pull out a packet of chewing gum, offer the other person a piece before taking one for yourself. Or when you want to pour yourself a cuppa coffee, offer to pour one for the other person first.

It's is different from the "put your oxygen mask on first before helping others" rule. Social graces are the norm unless it's an emergency. Even then, the captain goes down with the ship!

Stick with this rule. It's part of being the service-based leader we covered in the previous chapter. I've rubbed shoulders with some exceptionally successful business and social leaders, people in power who are held in high regard. No matter what industry they're in, there's always a common thread.

The higher up they are, the more gracious and elegant their demeanor. These people don't boast; they have no use for that. These men and women always have a smile and a kind word for others, whether it's the janitor or their CFO. They got where they are partially because of that attitude of service and compassion.

Take a moment and think about who you admire. It could be a relative or a world leader; it doesn't matter. It's the positive personal impact that counts. One of my favorites is Sir Richard Branson. I saw him speak live at an event in San Francisco and was quite taken by how gracious and down-to-earth he was. His parents instilled in his rebellious, entrepreneurial spirit good manners and solid ethics. The entire world respects him, and he's on a humanitarian mission for those in need in developing countries. He's authentic because he speaks from the heart. That's whose lead I choose to take.

You may find yourself in the company of people who don't think to offer their seat to an elderly person. That doesn't mean it's ok for you to slack off. You're on duty 24/7 to make the world a better place, one gesture at a time. Make sure that you uphold your own high standards. Know that others will take your lead and learn from you.

It can feel like a lot, all this work to make others feel comfortable, and there's enough decorum out there to sink an aircraft carrier. Like learning a new language, the idiosyncrasies are endless. The impetus goes so much deeper than that though. When you raise your own bar, you raise that of the people around you. It's the butterfly effect. Keep flapping those beautiful wings; it's worth every effort. Every wisp of wind makes a positive difference in the world.

I want to share some basics with you, so let's stick to the ones you're most likely to come across in your daily life: table manners. We all have to eat and dining together is a big part of everyone's business and personal lives.

But before we go there, because this book is primarily for men I have one extra poise pointer. It's for men who wear hats indoors, especially in restaurants. Here's where I'm compelled to go old school again. I don't care if you're a cowboy and you sleep in your Biltmore. It doesn't matter to me if you're betrothed to your baseball cap because you're sensitive about your bald spot. When you walk into a restaurant or anywhere indoors other than the gym or a barn, you remove your hat from your head.

You don't have to take it off when you greet a lady these days, but it would be awfully nice. Baseball caps are for kids and baseball players. They're also useful for keeping the sun out of your eyes while enjoying various sports. Aside from that, a grown man should never wear a baseball cap. It's neither sexy nor appropriate. There, I said it.

YOUR PUNCH LIST

Okay, now for the long-awaited must-know table manners:

- Want seconds of the mashed taters but you can't quite reach them? Ask someone to pass it to you. Never reach across the table or across anyone. It's ok, they'd rather pass it to you than get arm-blocked.
- Passing someone a dish? Set it down close to them, don't hand it to them. Less potential for spillage that way.
- Is something stuck in your teeth? Excuse yourself. No toothpicks at table or cupping your hand in front of your mouth while you excavate for a poppy seed with your fingernail.
- Got a runny nose or perhaps a bat stuck in the cave? Excuse yourself to go honk. Blowing your nose at table, especially into your napkin will make people gag. And digging for gold in your nose in front of anybody is downright disgusting.
- Elbows on the table? Don't get me started.
- Tired, tipsy and slumping? Sit up straight or go home if you can't right the ship.

Chick Magnet

- Want seconds of the mashed taters, but you can't quite reach them? Ask someone to pass it to you. Never reach across the table or across anyone. It's ok, they'd rather pass it to you than get arm-blocked.

- Passing someone a dish? Set it down close to them, don't hand it to them. Less potential for spillage that way.

- Is something stuck in your teeth? Excuse yourself. No toothpicks at the table or cupping your hand in front of your mouth while you excavate for a poppy seed with your fingernail.

- Got a runny nose or perhaps a bat stuck in the cave? Excuse yourself to go honk. Blowing your nose at the table, especially into your napkin will make people gag. And digging for gold in your nose in front of anybody is downright disgusting.

- Elbows on the table? Don't get me started.

- Tired, tipsy and slumping? Sit up straight or go home if you can't right the ship.

- Mouth full but have something colossal to say that you just can't keep in? Unless you see flames and you're about to shout "FIRE!!", swallow before speaking lest you shower the people you love with saliva encrusted steak moosh.

- Want to have more soufflé? Before you serve yourself, ask others if they'd like more, especially if supplies are low. The same goes for wine, share before you guzzle.
- Wondering where your hands should go when you're not eating? In North America, they go on your lap. In Europe, they go on the table. Good to know if you travel.
- Super hungry? Control your urge. Always wait for the host to dig in first before you do.
- Hot soup? No slurping or smacking. Unless you're under the age of two, eating should be silent.
- Ready for seconds? Wait until everyone has finished their plate before serving.
- All done and bored? Patience is a virtue. Wait until everyone is done eating before leaving the table.
- Napkin placement? On your lap. The moment you sit down, put it there. Don't wait until the vittles are served.
- Dining with a lady? Pull her chair in/out for her when she rises or sits.
- If your lady gets up to go powder her nose? You get up, sit down again. Do the same when she

returns. It'll feel weird at first, but it'll pay off in spades.

- What do you do with your fork and knife when done? Place them side by side in a 10 am to 4 pm position on your plate.
- Can't load those last morsels on your fork? Use your knife to push it on, never your finger; who knows where that thing's been.
- Having a hard time chopping a piece of food in two? Stop trying to sever it into two with your fork, that's what you knife is for. Use it.
- Is the host inclined to toast before eating? Wait before you guzzle. Sip on your water first if you're thirsty. Don't get caught with an empty wine glass before dinner starts.
- Making a point while holding a piece of cutlery? Avoid gesticulating with sharp objects in your hand. Someone could lose an eye if it's a particularly exciting story.
- Got a leathery hunk of ham on your plate? A backhanded fist stab with your fork will raise eyebrows. The tines of the fork should always be pointed from the fingertips, never from the bottom of the palm, Tarzan. That goes for you too, Jane.

- Is your cell phone buzzing up a storm in your purse or pocket? Suck it up, keep your phone on vibrate and tuck it away. You'll make others feel insignificant if your phone is even on the table. Unless you're a physician or nurse on call, it's inexcusable to check your phone at the table. Instead, excuse yourself to check it if you're expecting an urgent call or text.
- Above all, be appreciative and helpful. The host will forgive you anything if you help clear the table. Take it a step further and quietly change the garbage bag if it's getting full.

Wow, that's a mouthful! The whole M.O. behind these guidelines is to be considerate of others. I'm thankful for the strict upbringing my parents gave me. It was done with love, and it paved the path to greatness for me.

Good manner will get you places money won't.

There's lots more to this subject than can be covered in a couple of chapters but what you've learned so far will open many doors for you, I promise. You can thank me later!

Risk being seen in all your glory.

Jim Carrey

22

COMPLIMENTS, ANYONE?

I was handed a one-foot-square pine board at an event, and what happened next forever changed the way I look at things. It's a personal development event, and everyone is clutching their thin piece of wood. The speaker commands us: "Write your most limiting personal belief on the board." The crowd hushes. As people start searching their souls, some start sniffling back tears. Looking into the squirming pit of one's self-loathing beliefs can be disheartening —but sniffling? "What? Are these people all sissies?" I wonder to myself.

We're instructed to line up and one-by-one step onstage and punch through the board with our fist. Child's play. Of course, I'm perfect; I don't have any limiting beliefs. But I have to write something, so finally I scribble on the board and join the queue. The way I'm holding my board you'd think it was a winning hand in a high-stakes poker game.

Out of curiosity, I peer over the shoulder of one of the sniffling sissies to see what they wrote. Then I discretely start to read as many boards as I can make out. The common theme has me flabbergasted. About 80% of the boards read: "I'm not good enough" or "I'm not worthy."

"What's wrong with these people?" I think. Then I look down at my board. It reads, "I don't deserve." Oh, I didn't use to feel like this when I was a little kid. What happened?

The human journey had taken me for a wild ride. We go from being perfect as babies to feeling imperfect as we grow older. Then we move on to the perfection of dying. Along the way, we endure a cavalcade of losses and wins. Other people happen to us. Shit happens. Until we have the wisdom to know better, our knee-jerk reaction is to dish it back.

Somewhere along the journey, we take some hits that cripple our self-worth. I know I'm not alone when I share that my life is often a battle between outer conflict and inner peace. Overcoming the resistance, I feel to manifesting positive changes in my life is now part of my daily practice.

The way I defeat resistance is by encouraging others to acknowledge and embrace their strengths. I do this by giving them words of appreciation about their accomplishments and personal presence. They deserve it. We all do.

The funny thing is that at first, my praise is often met with push-back. People are uncomfortable accepting accolades, almost as if they are afraid to acknowledge their own attributes. If I didn't understand why some people downplay my laudation, I'd take offense. But I don't because I used to be the one who couldn't take a compliment.

Have you ever received a compliment and your automatic response was to say "Oh, this old thing? I found it in the trash." It was a long-standing joke between my mama and me. I'd say something like "nice shoes, ma" and she'd give me the trash line.

The "I'm not good enough" belief bars us from accepting a compliment. We don't feel we deserve the commendations, so we push them back. Anyway, isn't it conceited to think of how amazing we are? Why then, is the word "give" used with "compliment"? Makes you think. It's because a compliment is a gift given from the heart with sincerity.

There's a fine line between rebuffing a gift of praise and hurting someone's feelings. When we give someone something, we put ourselves in a vulnerable position. It's because it matters to us whether the other person will accept it with grace. After all, it's a heartfelt gift intended to make the other person feel appreciated. When we get the trash line in return, it can sting like a bee!

It's healthy to acknowledge to ourselves and others how awesome we are. It's got nothing to do with narcissism. It has everything to do with self-respect. Wouldn't you prefer to be around positive people who have a healthy self-esteem?

The next time someone pays you a compliment, just say "Thank you so much!" Now you're graciously accepting a gift from that person. If they handed you a bottle of the finest wine, wouldn't you thank them warmly? It wouldn't matter if you like wine or not; you'd never hand it back declaring, "I don't drink schlock." It's is no different.

In many cultures, it's considered extremely rude to turn down a gift. Think of an Italian mama continually filling your plate with pasta, "Mangia, mangia, you-a so skinny!" Imagine the look on her face were you to dare to decline another serving. "Mama mia, why you do thisa to me?"

In all fairness, the way a compliment is given can make a big difference in how it's received. Knowing how to give praise is a skill. One evening I was invited to a party at the home of a vivacious couple. It was an upscale affair, so I wore a flowing silk dress and pair of sexy stilettos. That evening I was turning heads. At one point I was sitting next to Alex, the host. He was intently searching his iPod for a good dance playlist when he leaned over to show me something on the device.

When I leaned in to look, he said, "You know you're smoking hot, don't you?" Alex is so charismatic and fun that if he were single, I'd go out with him in a heartbeat. But he's happily married, and we're friends. The question made me think.

"I do, thank you, Alex" I responded, my wheels turning.

He explained, "You know, I work with a lot of women, and I struggle to give compliments to them without being misinterpreted. I love to give praise, and I don't mean it in a sexual way. I'm showing them my appreciation for making the extra effort to take care of themselves."

I was relieved to hear him say that because I did wonder for a moment. Now I knew it wasn't intended to be lewd. I wouldn't have to worry that his lovely wife would come at me with a meat cleaver and change the way I part my hair. That would have been a pity because I so enjoy their company.

I had to think before responding because if a friend's husband were to flatter me in a lascivious way, I would no longer be able to accept invitations from them. So I decided to offer Alex some advice on how to safely pay that kind of a compliment in the future. He was ready to listen. I offered because I also love to compliment men for being their ultimate best.

You can tell when a guy is genuine. He'll go out of his way to be respectful of others and himself and stand out from the crowd. I'll notice him immediately. I love to tell such men how handsome they look or how well put together they are. For them not to take my praise the wrong way, I'll preface it with "May I pay you a compliment?" It works like a charm!

> "Women are never disarmed by compliments. Men always are. That is the difference between the sexes."
>
> —Oscar Wilde

I did it in Tampa when I was attending a leadership event. I was strolling the riverside walk and slipped into a lively bistro for some vittles. I bellied up to the bar, the best place to get quick service. When I looked over to the bartender, he smiled at me. My heart skipped a beat.

The man was stunningly drop-dead breathtakingly gorgeous. Stop laughing; he was hot! However, I did not wish to lure him back to my room. Boy, I had such an urge to tell him how impressive he was! I knew I had to let 'er rip because otherwise I'd keep staring at him and embarrass myself.

"Excuse me; I'd love a Jim Beam Black on the rocks. By the way, may I pay you a compliment, please?" I asked, peeling my tongue off the bar. "Of course," said the Adonis barman. I gave him this: "You are so handsome, you're a pleasure to look at. Thank you for taking such excellent care of yourself." He took it exactly as intended. I was able to take my eyes off him because he'd accepted my gift graciously. That evening I got the best service ever.

Sometimes a compliment can be too much or inappropriate. One of my clients, David, who had come to me for an image overhaul, was suffering from the Nice Guy Syndrome — meaning he had plenty of female friends, but couldn't get a single one to date him.

Regrettably, David was so comfortable in his "why don't women want a nice guy" but that he was unwilling to do the work on himself to change the tides. A loss for womankind because he is a gem.

One of the problems with David was that he habitually over-complimented women he was interested in. I knew this because I was often on the receiving end. He'd frequently call or text saying things like, "How's the sexiest, most beautiful woman in the world?"

As a standalone, that could work, but it happened way too often. It had become a turn-off that made me want to avoid him. It got embarrassing for me because I'd expressly never signaled romantic interest to him. I don't dip my pen in the company ink.

I felt like he was putting me on a goddess pedestal. From that lofty perch, I began to lose respect for David because his behavior belied a lack of self-worth. "Be normal, stop bowing. I'm a real woman, not a mythical creature," I wanted to tell him. It's too much pressure, and it gets old fast because there's no challenge. Put someone on a pedestal, and their interest in you will soon wane because you've just placed your confidence in the basement. Remember that confidence is sexy, so don't bury it. Let it shine for all to see!

People want to be appreciated for who they are, not someone else's fantasy of them. Be sincere and authentic with your adulations.

Be careful to send the right message. Don't sell the farm with excessive accolades. When you go on a date with someone, pay them one compliment. More is overkill. Keep it up, and your date will eventually stop returning your calls and texts. That's great if you're a masochist. I'd rather be out having fun with a date than pace around at home, checking my phone to see if it's still working.

On the flip side, there are those who don't bequeath recognition at all. Heaven forbid they should risk being vulnerable. It's their loss because they're usually the ones who need praise the most, yet they're too afraid to let down their guard and give the gift of a bon mot.

A woman needs to know that the energy she puts into looking her best is appreciated. It's nice to be acknowledged for that. She has a lot more steps than you to take before she steps out. Say something — one thing.

A man who puts a lot of energy into being and doing his best can also use a little praise. A simple "Wow, you really know to drive. I feel completely safe with you at the wheel" works wonders.

If you're the kind of person who doesn't compliment, think about changing your ways. Remember a man named Scrooge? Wasn't he rather lonely and single? Just fork it over and give a little!

A compliment is the currency of compassion. Spend it wisely.

Imagine you have so much cash that you line your birdcage with hundred dollar bills. Now imagine meeting a destitute old soul sitting on park bench. You give them ten of those bills because there's plenty more where that came from. They hesitate, not knowing what to do because you've moved them. Finally, they take the money and croak "Thank you so much; I haven't eaten in days."

Doesn't it feel wonderful to see their face light up? It's the same feeling when you lift someone up by offering a well-deserved word of praise. You're giving from the heart — there's no substitute for that.

When it comes to appropriately doling out compliments, my mama was the ultimate role model. She'd give them frequently but selectively. Among the recipients were cashiers, her yoga instructor Burt, the nurse who looked after her in the hospital, anyone whom she appreciated. She had the knack of combining a compliment with a word of appreciation. It was brilliant.

When you applaud someone this way, you're explaining to that person how their extra effort is benefitting you! It makes it so much easier for them to accept your gift.

Even when mama was no longer able to walk, she kept the kind words coming. You could feel the warmth in her heart even when she was fading. It shone from her eyes and slipped past her smile, "That was just the ticket, Burt, thank you for the great yoga class."

The last and most important step is adding the reason you're praising them.

Giving a compliment equals offering appreciation; it gets even better when you add why you appreciate their effort. That's why, right after I told the hot stuff bartender in Tampa how handsome he was, I explained it was a pleasure to look at him. I even thanked him for taking good care of himself. He loved it and felt he was of service to me beyond being a great bartender. He realized he was improving the view for me and that made him smile on the inside.

By praising someone and telling them why you're doing it, you're thanking them for improving your enjoyment of life. You're acknowledging that they're worthy of being loved and that they have done you a service.

YOUR PUNCH LIST

If you're uncomfortable handing out compliments, that's okay; there's still hope. You can get there by taking baby steps toward mindfulness.

Do these exercises in the following order:

1. Offer small bits of praise to people you don't know well.

    - The checkout clerk at the grocery store.
    - The janitor at work.
    - A stranger in line next to you at theater concession stand.

2. Now move on up to people you know better.

    - Your hairdresser.
    - A coworker.
    - Your personal trainer.
    - A rival.
    - Someone you despise.

3. It's time to graduate to those closer to you.

    - Friends.
    - Relatives.
    - Lovers.

Chick Magnet

From now on, eliminate the awkwardness others feel when faced with a compliment. Give them a reason to accept it; they've done you a service! It's a reciprocal act. Instead of dropping a hot potato in their hands you're giving them oven mitts with which to hold it.

Now get out there and pay it forward!

Look at what a man could be and that is what he will become.

Les Brown

23

NOW WHAT?

I was exploring a quiet beach near a remote fishing village in Mexico when a tow-headed boy came running up to me out of nowhere. He had braces on his teeth, and his red baseball cap was perched backward atop his shaggy mane. What he said utterly caught me off guard.

Gasping for air after his sandy gallop, the freckle-faced lad panted, "Hi. Can I have your phone number?" "Why?" I asked. "Uh..." was all he could muster before racing back to a group of adults lounging in white plastic chairs at a tiny beach restaurant. It took me by surprise because he couldn't have been more than ten years old.

"Boy, they're getting younger all the time!" I silently mused. Then I realized he was likely on a dare. Good for him! If only he'd stuck around I would've gladly given him a few pointers for the future. For one, he could have kept me talking a bit longer by asking me a question, like "Hey, do you see those dolphins swimming over there?"

Reflecting on this, I realized that while my mission is to help single adult males achieve the love life, they dream of, the information I share would benefit boys from the moment they start looking at girls as more than just playmates.

To all the men who dove into these chapters with an open mind and heart, I honor you. You've done yourself a huge favor because now that you've gotten inside her head, the dating game is going to make a whole lot more sense.

Have you ever had the experience of reading a book for the second time and finding valuable nuggets that eluded you the first time? That's because your perspective has shifted a bit and you're ready for more in-depth learning. I'm reminding you of this because I want you to obtain as much clarity as possible from this book. I invite you to read the whole book more than once and to refer to specific chapters often.

This book is more than a lexicon of pick-up lines and get-her-into-the-sack quick tricks. It's about learning how to approach, attract and build an authentic relationship with that someone special. You can apply many of the same skills you learn from this book to building relationships in social and business situations.

Your inner critic may be saying:

- I've been in a rut for so long.
- I always end up stuck in the friend zone while the other guys get the girl.
- As a single dad, I'll never find time to date.
- She's out of my league, and she'll just turn me down.
- I don't know what to say; why even bother approaching her?

- Women don't find me sexually attractive.

That's your inner bodyguard tugging at your sleeve, trying to protect you from apparent danger. Tell it to go sit on the bench. You've got this.

The three sections in this book have given you the tools and the "female" perspective to move beyond that mindset:

Section 1

YOU — Develop your personal skills.

Chick Magnet

- You've mastered the art of confidently approaching women, and quickly making a physical and emotional connection.
- You've learned exactly how to get women to want you because they see you as the fascinating, exciting man that you are.
- She'll feel safe in your arms because you've revealed both your bold and your vulnerable sides in just the right measure.

Section 2

HER — Understand things from her perspective.

- You now know what's important to single women and you work it.
- You know why it matters because you've heard it from your female dating coach.
- You've practiced what you've learned and have seen results.

Section 3

THE BIG PICTURE — Fine-tune your etiquette skills in any social setting.

- This section is priceless because you never know who you'll meet at the next shindig.

- Here's the bonus part — you've learned some key social skills to use with others — anytime, anywhere.

My papa inspired *Chick Magnet*. He was a brilliant, incredibly handsome man, and during his 60-year marriage to my mama, he struggled to fathom her female mind. While I did my best to help, I don't know if he ever fully understood how she thought. Nor did she fully understand him. It was another era, and things were different. I wish he could have read this book. No doubt they are now sipping fine French champagne together in the hereafter and musing about their human journey together.

Please don't wait that long to co-create a fulfilling, passionate, happy love life. Pass it on! If you have a son, teach him the basics you've learned here. Explain to him how men's and women's minds work. Teach him to be insightful, respectful and gentlemanly at an early age. If you have a daughter, the best way you can educate her about dating is to teach her about how a man thinks and why — and how to be a lady and let the man be the man. She'll need to learn how to weed out the bad boys at an early age. Why wait until her first date rings your doorbell?

You're armed with the right information and tips now, and your confidence with women is inspired because you have clarity, and clarity is power. You've learned to master and use your fear positively. There's no need to try to read a woman's mind, now that you know how to read the signals she sends with her body language, voice, and words. And you know how to respond to those signals. The guesswork is gone. Knowing the difference between what a woman wants and what she needs gives you a big head start on the competition. Act accordingly, and you'll succeed in getting what you want and need, both in and out of the bedroom.

Give her what she wants *and* needs - a combination of confident and nice: brave, intelligent, edgy, selfless, honest, compassionate.

But above all, get this: The secret sauce to getting the girl is to incorporate the information I've provided and the above qualities with your own unique personality. Be your highest, most authentic self, make the utmost of what God gave you and let the chips fall where they may. It will always steer you right. Getting women to crave you takes more than just understanding how they think: it takes realizing that you are half the equation of any relationship.

See what you could be, do the work, and you will become the ultimate, most irresistible version of yourself.

Be bold and put yourself out there. The ball's in your court. Ask yourself: "What steps am I going to take today, right now, to become a Chick Magnet?"

Now go forth confidently, step into the arena, and claim your love life!

ADDITIONAL RESOURCES

For more information and products on how to attract women, check out our blog at thedatingmuse.com. Ask about our personal coaching programs and products. Get on our mailing list, so you don't miss a thing. We promise we won't flood your inbox.

Many thanks to my book coach, Les Kletke. I am eternally grateful to him for his patience, expertise and unorthodox sense of humor. Do you have a book inside you that needs to get out? Email Les at lkletke@mymts.net, and tell him I sent you.

He who would begun has half done. Dare to be wise; begin.

Horace

YOUR PUNCH LIST SUMMARY

Part 1: YOU

Are you wondering how to answer that last question, "What steps am I going to take today, right now, to become a Chick Magnet?" I know I've given you a lot to take in — so this last chapter is devoted to making the process as smooth as possible for you.

What follows is a summary of every punch list in this book.

Follow these pointers, and you'll be well on your way to:

- Ensuring you make a stellar impression every time you walk into a room.
- Knowing precisely what steps to take to enter the dating arena with conviction, and claim your love life!

Thank you for diving into this book with an open mind. Congratulations on finishing it and taking action, because she's out there waiting for you — and now, you're oceans ahead of the pack!

1

THE IMPORTANCE OF FIRST IMPRESSIONS

Facial hair:

- If you choose to have a beard or mustache, it is imperative that you keep it neatly trimmed and shaped.
- Stubble can cause a painful rash on a woman's chin when engaging in passionate kisses. If she gets a rash and you like her, start shaving.
- A mustache should be trimmed so it doesn't reach below the top of the lip line. We ladies want to feel your soft lips, not facial hair in our mouth when we kiss you.
- Trim nose hair and parsley ears regularly. Battery-operated trimmers can be found at the drug store.
- The "weekend" scruff is not a good idea for a first date. Keep neatly trimmed if you do sport it.
- Short hair should be trimmed every 4 to 5 weeks. Trim sideburns and shave back of neck every

week to keep your cut looking neat. Shave stray hairs on your upper cheeks.

- Keep your nails, all twenty of them neatly trimmed and filed. Save yourself a whole lot of hangnails and crusty feet repulsion. If you have calloused feet, go get a pedicure. I'm serious!

- Wash your hair several times a week to keep your head smelling fresh. Rinse conditioner through in-between if your scalp is dry.

- Always style your hair. Consult your hairdresser for suggestions.

Your kisser:

- Tooth are crooked, get them straightened. Uneven or damaged teeth can spoil an otherwise sexy smile.

- Brush and floss meticulously to prevent bad breath.

Your style:

- Wardrobe — Fit and quality is critical, and believe it or not, women want to see the shape of your rear.

- Consult with a stylist/wardrobe expert to help develop a personal style that will make her want to undress you. Stick with your new style.

- Match the outfit to the occasion. Except for fashion sneakers, avoid running shoes at all times unless you are either going to, at, or coming from a workout, or she'll cringe thinking about what you'll wear.

#

2

THE LANGUAGE OF THE BODY

To project confidence:

- Smile more — it's been scientifically proven that it:
  - **Makes you attractive to others.** There is an automatic attraction to people who smile.

  - **Improves your mood.** Try, even when it's difficult, to smile when you are feeling low.

There is a good chance it will improve the way you're feeling.

- **Is contagious.** In a good way, others will want to be with you. You will be helping others feel good.
- **Relieves stress.** When we smile, it can help us feel better, less tired, less worn down.
- **Boosts the immune system.** Smiling can stimulate your immune response by helping you relax.
- **Lowers blood pressure.** When you smile, there is evidence that your blood pressure can decrease.
- **Releases endorphins and serotonin.** Research has reported that smiling releases endorphins, which are natural pain relievers, along with serotonin, which is also associated with feeling good.

How you carry yourself is equally important in displaying confident body language. Here are some habit changing how-tos:

- Study your reflection in the mirror and observe your posture. Are you standing straight? Are you leading with the heart?

Chick Magnet

- Is your upper body leaning back from the person you're talking to? Align your shoulders over your hips to look more confident.
- Be conscious of how you sit at your desk. Are your back and shoulders hunched? Straighten them and keep checking in with yourself regularly until sitting and standing straight become a habit.
- Are you craning your neck forward because you need glasses? Get some cool ones. Craning puts a tremendous strain on your neck and makes you appear insecure. Bonus: studies indicate that women are attracted to men wearing stylish glasses.
- Are you fiddling with your hands when speaking with people? You may be nervous, but you don't want to advertise it. Calm your hands and separate them from one another.
- Keep your hands out of your pockets. There is nothing to hide, and it conveys disinterest.
- Avoid crossing your arms in unconscious self-defense. Keep them at your sides, odd as this may feel.
- Clasping your hands in front of your groin or behind your rear are signs of fear and emotional discomfort. No one is going to kick you there. Again, practice keeping your hands at your sides.

#

3

YOUR EYES SAY WHAT YOUR WORDS DON'T

Mastering eye contact:

- First, look into her eyes for about five seconds. It'll feel like an eternity but the length of time you lock eyes with her matters.
- Slowly put a twinkle in your eye by lifting the corners of your mouth. Friendly is good, and it will disarm her for now.
- Give her a slight nod to acknowledge her.
- Repeat in a couple of minutes.

#

4

WHEN YOU OPEN YOUR MOUTH

Review your selfie video recordings and observe yourself. Do an honest self-assessment. You'll start to notice where you sound and looks more confident, more engaging:

- Ask yourself, "Where can I improve? Which delivery is most charismatic? Would I want to hang out with me?"
- Practice it a thousand times if you have to. It works.
- Watch yourself after each time and note where there is room for improvement; you want to capture her attention and admiration with your voice and your overall delivery.
- Work at it. Each time it'll be better, I promise.
- Now pick an exciting anecdote to work on and memorize — be prepared for your next female encounter.

#

5

FIRST WORDS

Here's how to be a great conversationalist

- Skip a beat and engage her in some playful banter first.
- Next, talk about some personal tender moments, passionate moments, joyful moments. (Not ones about former love interests!) Talk about what you love and use the word, love.
- Let that emotion show in your voice, on your face and in your body language.
- Use enthusiasm and passion when you speak — fill her with anticipation and excitement.
- Now, with that momentum, get your Fantastic Four across.
- Always, always, always ask her about her special moments; coax her to describe them and how she felt.

- Get your foot in the door!

When asking her on a date, give her no more than three options from which to choose. Always be prepared with the following three strategies:

- Plan A
- Backup plan B
- Backup, backup plan C

#

6

FIRST TOUCH

Here are the steps for introducing yourself to strangers; follow them in this order:

- Make eye contact. Maintain it as you approach the person, during the handshake and afterward. Keep your head up. Do not look at the ground.
- Smile. Always start with a small smile and let it grow on your face as you approach.

- Say "Hi, my name is ______". If the other person doesn't offer their name, ask their name after saying yours. Start speaking a split second before you reach out your hand.
- Shake their hand for 1–2 second with just the right firmness, using the web-to-web grip.

#

7

THE SEXIEST QUALITY OF ALL

Here are some places to practice you bantering skills with women:

- Here are some places to practice you bantering skills with women:
- Volunteer somewhere where your preferred kind of woman is also likely to volunteer, e.g., church, homeless shelter, boys and girls club, Rotary Club, etc. You'll showcase your emotional caring perfectly this way.

- Attend improv classes. I can't say enough about this. It'll skyrocket your quick-wittedness and ability to drum up a humorous conversation.
- Join Toastmasters, learn how to converse concisely and confidently.
- Join social clubs and meet-ups that revolve around your interests.
- Join a co-ed team sports activity such as volleyball, a rowing club or tennis club. Something you genuinely enjoy.

#

8

PHYSICAL TOUCH

Here's how to play your petting cards right:

- Start slowly.
- Pay attention.
- Savor the moments.

- Push a bit further when you feel it's appropriate.
- Pull back slightly if she does, to the same degree.
- Lather rinse, repeat.

#

9

SILENT ATTRACTION SIGNALS

From now on, when you see female prospects, look for these Silent Attraction Signals that indicate she's interested in you:

- When you catch her eye, if she likes you, she looks down or to the side. Looking up at the ceiling means "move on."
- She starts giggling with her friends when you make eye contact.
- She touches any part of herself, adjusts clothing, plays with her necklace, hair, etc.

- She strokes her glass or straw. I'm serious!
- She smiles back at you. Hello!
- She looks away and then peeks back within 45 seconds.

#

10

WHY WOMEN WANT BAD BOYS

Here's how to walk the post-date communication fine line between being both a nice guy and a bad-ass alpha male:

- Avoid overwhelming your love interests with an overload of affection and texts too early on in the game. Be cool.
- Have a relatively strict set of guidelines, always follow up after a date and say "Thanks, I had a nice time", even if you're not interested.

- After that, at least in the beginning — it should be a one for one. Text her and wait for a reply.
- Understand pace. Not everyone has their phone glued to their forehead. Some may take hours to respond; others may be immediate. Chill.
- Gauge interest on her part.
- Do not over-communicate by bombarding her with texts, pictures, emails, phone calls, etc. You'll appear desperate and needy. You want her to crave you not shake you off.
- After things get rolling, be less concerned about waiting for a reply. You might send a couple of texts in a row if an exciting things strike you.
- Always monitoring for/steer clear of neediness in your tone and texts..

Part 2: HER

11

HER SIDE

Keep her point of view in your mind when you:

- Decide on what to wear for date.
- Shop for *quality* clothing, shoes, underwear, (yes it matters).
- Choose a cologne. Not too strong.
- Visit you hairdresser. Don't skimp, you get what you pay for.
- Are about to toss that double bacon cheeseburger wrapper into the back seat of your car? Think again.
- Leave the toilet seat up. Down boy.
- Think of skipping the gym. Uh-uh.
- Wonder if you should invest in a housekeeper.

12

HER GOALS

- **Be aware of your dating goals**
  - If your goals are to date around for a while and sample different women, that's absolutely fine! It's the best thing to do after a divorce, when exiting a long-term relationship or when widowed. Rebound relationships are always bound for a cul-de-sac because you're not the same man you were when you entered your last relationship. Avoid making the same mistake twice.

- **Be honest with her *and* with yourself**
  - Be honest with your dates about your dating goals. Take the time to figure out what you want. If you're dating around merely looking for a good time, that's cool, but tell her. If she's looking for a long-term relationship, cool it. If she has kids or wants kids and that's not your thing, back off because right out of the gate it's not a good match.

- **Take care of the grooming details**
  - Why ruin your chances? Start by checking out your hands and feet. Take care of this business if you want her to desire you. Admit

it; there's nothing quite like having the woman you want, desire you. The mutual sexual attraction is like a drug. And that is never truer than it is at the beginning of a relationship. Trust me; this work is all worth it!

#

13

LITTLE THINGS ADD UP

Try to see yourself from your date's perspective — check off these essential items on your "before you leave your place" list:

- Get a full-length mirror, hang it by your front door.
- Before you check out of your place, check yourself out.
- Inspect yourself:
    - Shoes shined?
    - Facial hair trimmed/shaved, any missed patches?

- Nose/ear hairs weed-whacked?
- Any missing buttons?
- Loose threads?
- Any stains, signs of wear on clothing?
- Any wardrobe malfunctions, e.g., pant leg accidentally stuck in a sock, shirt tucked into underpants, flying low, socks matching?
- **If you can't fix whatever's amiss in two minutes, don't ignore it. Put something else on.**
- Hands/nails looking good?
- Hair clean and styled?
- Bits of reuben-on-rye sandwich removed from between your teeth?
- Breath fresh?

- Before your date, practice mental preparation and visualization like this:
    - Rehearse the date in your mind.
    - Where are you going?

- What will you talk about? What have you discovered about her that you want to learn more about?
- What words will you use to create an emotional zip-line with her?
- How will you touch her?
- How do you want to present yourself?
- Feeling less than your best? Give yourself a personal pep talk on the way over to perk up.
- Remind yourself that you're a good man, charming, witty, etc. by recalling evidence of that.

#

14

CHIVALRY IS KING

Here's how to tweak your behavior to be a *real* man:

- Pay for date expenses for the first few dates, then play it by ear, e.g., cook for her. It's not about how much you spend. Find fun, wallet-friendly places to take her, like a free outdoor concert or group dance lessons.

- If you've let her pull out her wallet, it's too late.
- Be sure to make the first move to offer help. You are the alpha-man, not her.
- Reach out first when you want to help her, but be aware of how she reacts and make sure she's comfortable with it.
- If she's hesitant to accept it, offer help in small increments. Be persistent, be consistent, in a measured way.
- Don't smother her from the get-go. Gradually start doing sweet little things for her. It'll show her you care.
- When walking on the sidewalk with her, always take the curbside.

#

15

LANDING & EXECUTING THE FIRST DATE

When you go talk to a honey bunny your goal should be three-part

1. Gather information on her preferences when you strike up the conversation.

2. Casually give her the low-down on the Fantastic Four things she needs to know about you that we covered in Chapter 5. Essential to have her feel at ease about you.

3. Have two to three options in mind when you ask her the big question "May I take you out to the firing range, parachuting, an acrobatic show...

#

16

INVITE HER OVER

Here's how to make your place inviting for your date:

- Barring a blizzard, air your place out thoroughly for at least an hour before your date arrives. Especially if you have pets. You may not notice how stale air can sink into the furniture but she will. Don't take a chance on this one, especially in the bedroom!
- Every room that she might enter should be clean, tidy and fresh-smelling. Don't use those stinky, toxic air fresheners; they are tell-tale. Just air the place out, and try some Nag Champa incense.
- Pay particular attention to your bedroom and your bedding. Should she be feeling amorous your sheets had better be clean and, your bed freshly made.
- Light a few aromatic candles about half an hour before her arrival. Stick with a comforting warm vanilla or nutty scent for now. Works wonders.
- The most significant word here is — clean! The sight of clutter and junk lying around will have her forever unavailable to you. If house cleaning's not

your thing, hire someone to do the dirty work for you.

- Go to great lengths to keep your breath fresh. Here's how:
- Avoid not just the obvious — onions, garlic, salami, smoking, etc., that day and the day before.
- On the day of your date also avoid beer, red wine, sugary foods, sodas strong cheeses and other pungent foods. To a woman, bad breath is the death knell as far as smooching goes.
- Drink plenty of water — about eight glasses a day will help flush toxins that can cause halitosis. Choose water over juices and sugary, flavored drinks to help meet the quota and keep your breath fresh. Caffeinated and alcoholic beverages don't count — they'll dehydrate you. Even diet colas will cause your breath to be uninviting. Breath mints can temporarily mask things when in doubt, but don't leave them in view. Women notice the details.

#

17

SEDUCE HER WITH COOKING

Before you cook for/with her, read this:

- Ask about her food preferences ahead of time. Dietary restrictions run aplenty — asking shows you're conscientious.
- Pick up a lovely wine that pairs well with the dish. It doesn't have to be expensive, don't bring cheap schlock. If you're not sure what to get, go to an adult beverage store and ask an expert. If she's cooking and you don't know what the dish is, a nice bottle of Prosecco or champagne will be the perfect icebreaker.
- Have fresh ingredients and keep the recipe simple. This way you'll be able to talk because your mind won't be preoccupied.
- If cooking at her place, make sure you have all the ingredients you'll need OR ask if she has them at her home, e.g., olive oil, vinegar.
- Clean up after yourself so she can feel reassured that you're organized and respectful. If she offers

to wash up, doing dishes together can be lots of fun! Clean the dishes thoroughly — remember Sergey?

- Wipe off counters, pick up any fallen food lest it gets smooshing underfoot. No need to be anal, just do a good job.

#

18

ASK FOR THE SALE

Follow this Perfect Timing Technique checklist to know when to ask for her number:

- Make your move sooner than you think you should, but not right away. Talking al evening with only her in hopes you'll eventually rally the courage to ask her out will dull the initial impact of your introduction. You may be keeping her from her friends, and you'll be more likely to mess things up.

Chick Magnet

- Find out early on if she's eligible, discreetly. Avoid burning a whole night talking only to find out she has a boyfriend or separated yesterday.

- Behave as if you're popular, even if you're not. Introduce yourself to some groups of both guys and gals. You want her to see you talking with other people. It demonstrates you have social intelligence.

- Find out what she likes.

- Check her body language. Is her body opening up to you? Is she making eye contact, smiling at you, facing you?

- Do you get that feeling she's into you, fully engaged? Or is she distracted and looking around for someone to rescue her?

- Touch her gently before you ask for her number. Make that electric physical connection. You know what to do, upper arm, shoulder, middle of the back. Plug into her and get her oxytocin flowing.

- Think of a place to take her she'll enjoy.

- Whammo! Now it's time to ask her. "There's a new dance studio I'd love to take you to for a salsa class!"

- She accepts, you get her number. Ka-ching.

- Call her within two days of meeting and touching her.

To ensure your voice resonates with a rich, relaxed tone rather than a shaky squeak when you talk to the ladies, do this quick meditation before moving in:

- While focusing on your breath, slowly inhale for seven counts right down into your belly. Hold at the top for a few seconds. Then slowly exhale for eight counts with your jaw relaxed and your mouth slightly ajar.
- Repeat this three times.
- Relax your eyelids till they are almost bedroom eyes, keep them that way to appear relaxed. Nothing wrong with the bedroom. It will help prevent the "Charles Manson in the headlights" eyes.
- Practice the above when talking to people in general. See how much more relaxed you feel and notice the difference in the response you get.

#

19

GOLD DIGGER OR REALIST

To attract classy, beautiful women who are not gold diggers, emulate the men you respect. Start with this:

- Stride confidently — you never know who's watching.
- Stand tall and proud — whether you're 5′6″ or 6′5″.
- Work hard and smart — be bound for success with every fiber in your body.
- Never complain — take responsibility for yourself; it's a sign of a real leader.
- Take the high road — there's no upside in taking someone else's poor behavior personally.
- If you haven't got anything nice to say about someone, don't say anything — now that's class.
- Lead from a place of service — you get respect when you give it.
- Work hard and smart at improving yourself — curiosity is sexy.

- Surround yourself with the right people — you'll attract the right women.
- Curtail your cuss words — the right woman may pass you by if you don't.
- Do the paradigm shift — you don't have to tell her everything but look at her side of the coin if she asks about your finances.

#

Part 3: THE BIG PICTURE

20

THE LEADER

To become a good leader, practice the exercises below on a daily basis:

- Go above and beyond the call of duty in everything you do.
- Do it with a smile, be a service-based leader.
- Practice random acts of kindness.
- Don't tell others that you did it.
- Act with integrity and empathy in every little thing you do.
- Have a kind word of affirmation for everyone — the boss, the person in the wheelchair, the person you hate.
- Show respect for yourself and others by taking superb care of yourself.
- Take the initiative even when the task is unpleasant.

- Do the unexpected for others.
- Be a giver, not a taker.
- Work hard and smart.
- Be respectful.
- When you fall down, get back up.
- Take responsibility for yourself, don't blame your misgivings on others.
- Surround yourself with exceptional people.
- Remember that no one is better than you, and you're not better than anyone else.

#

21

GOOD MANNERS

Familiarize yourself with these must-know table manners:

- Familiarize yourself with these must-know table manners:

- If you want seconds but can't quite reach the dish, ask someone to pass it to you. Never reach across the table or across anyone.
- To pass someone a dish, set it down close to them, don't hand it to them.
- No toothpicks at the table or cupping your hand in front of your mouth while you pick your teeth with your fingernail.
- Avoid blowing your nose at the table, especially into your napkin. Instead, excuse yourself to the bathroom.
- Keep your elbows off the table.
- Sit up straight.
- Avoid speaking while food is in your mouth, swallow first.
- Before you serve yourself, ask others if they'd like more, especially if supplies are low. The same goes for wine.
- In North America, your hands go on your lap at the table. In Europe, they go on the table.
- Always wait for the host to dig in first before you do.
- No slurping or smacking of any kind.

Chick Magnet

- Wait until everyone has finished their plate before serving.
- Wait until everyone is done eating before leaving the table.
- Place your napkin on your lap the moment you sit down.
- Dining with a lady? Pull her chair in/out for her when she rises or sits.
- When your lady gets up to go powder her nose, you get up, sit down again. Do the same when she returns.
- When done eating, place your fork them side by side in a 10 am to 4 pm position on your plate.
- Always use your knife to push food onto your fork, never your finger.
- Use your knife to cut your food, not your fork.
- If the host inclined to toast before eating, wait before draining your glass. Don't get caught with an empty wine glass before dinner starts.
- Avoid gesticulating with eating utensils in your hand.
- The tines of your fork should always be pointed from the fingertips, never from the bottom of the palm.

- Keep your phone on vibrate and tuck it away, never place it on the dining table. Excuse yourself if you're expecting an urgent call or text.
- Be appreciative and helpful. Help clear the table — offer help to clean up further.

#

22

COMPLIMENTS, ANYONE?

Practice giving compliments in this order:

1. Offer small bits of praise to people you don't know well.
    - The checkout clerk at the grocery store.
    - The janitor at work.
    - A stranger in line next to you at the theater concession stand.
2. Now move on up to people you know better.
    - Your hairdresser.

- A coworker.
- Your personal trainer.
- A rival.
- Someone you despise.

3. It's time to graduate to those closer to you.
    - Friends.
    - Relatives.
    - Lovers.

ADDITIONAL RESOURCES

For more info on approaching women check out this video: How to Approach a Woman. https://thedatingmuse.mykajabi.com/blog/tips-on-how-to-approach-women

For more tips on men's style, check out my interview with author and expert in the sociology of style Anna Akbari Ph.D., How to Use Style to Attract Women. https://thedatingmuse.mykajabi.com/blog/Using_Style

Many thanks to my book coach, Les Kletke. I am eternally grateful to him for his patience, expertise and unorthodox sense of humor. Much gratitude for my dear friend, Phil, and my editor, Brenda Conroy, who saw everything I didn't!

Do you have a book inside you that needs to get out? Email Les at lkletke@mymts.net and tell him I sent you.

ENDNOTES

2

[1] Amy Cuddy. "Your Body Language May Shape Who You Are." *TED*, June, 20012. https://www.ted.com/talks/amy_cuddy_your_body_language_shapes_who_you_are?language=en

3

[2] Joss Fong. "Eye-Opener: Why Do Pupils Dilate in Response to Emotional States." *Scientific American*, December 7, 2012. https://www.scientificamerican.com/article/eye-opener-why-do-pupils-dialate/

[3] Mandy Len Catron. "To Fall in Love With Anyone, Do This." *The New York Times*, January 9, 2015. www.nytimes.com/2015/01/11/fashion/modern-love-to-fall-in-love-with-anyone-do-this.html?_r=0

[4] Farlax. *The Free Dictionary. "Can You Really Improve Your Emotional Intelligence?"* Harvard Business Review, http://www.thefreedictionary.com/staring

5

[5] Tomas Chamorro-Premuzic. "Can You Really Improve Your Emotional Intelligence?" *Harvard Business Review,* May 29, 2013. https://hbr.org/2013/05/can-you-really-improve-your-em

6

[6] Michelle Trudeau. "Human Connections Start With A Friendly Touch." *NPR,* September 20, 2010. http://www.npr.org/templates/story/story.php?storyId=128795325

[7] Roz Usheroff, Leadership, Image and Branding Specialist. "How to overcome making a bad first impression." *LinkedIn*, April 23, 2014. https://www.linkedin.com/pulse/article/20140424005629-3411076-how-to-overcome-making-a-bad-first-impression

[8] Jessica Stillman. "9 Ways to Fix a Bad First Impression." *Inc.* http://www.inc.com/jessica-stillman/9-ways-to-fix-a-bad-first-impression.html

8

[9] Michelle Trudeau. "Human Connections Start With A Friendly Touch." *NPR,* September 20, 2010.

http://www.npr.org/templates/story/story.php?storyId=128795325

15

[10] Mark B. Kastleman. *The Drug of the New Millennium: The Science of How Internet Pornography Radically Alters the Human Brain and Body,* 2007. PowerThink Publishing.

16

[11] Will Wister, published writer, *HuffPost, Time, Forbes, Medical Daily, The Atlantic, and Lifehacker* "Do women have a more acute sense of smell than men?" https://www.quora.com/Do-women-have-a-more-acute-sense-of-smell-than-men/answer/Will-Wister, November 20, 2013.

20

[12] Ecole Polytechnique Federale de Lausanne. "The First Ever Photograph of Light as Both a Particle and Wave." *phys.org,* March 2, 2015. https://m.phys.org/news/2015-03-particle.html

Endnotes

REFERENCES

The following references served the author immensely in her literature reviews for this project. Although the Author did not cite every resource in the endnotes of this book, each informed the work and the author's supplemental research articles on **thedatingmuse.com**. The Author wishes to thank all the researchers and practitioners and friends whether noted here or not, who generously provided their expertise and insight for this book. They have helped her to inspire all men to pursue excellence within themselves and within their love lives.

Johnson, Robert A.(1991). *Owning Your Own Shadow: Understanding the Dark Side of the Psyche.* New York, NY: HarperCollins Publishers Inc.

Pressfield, Steven (2002). *The war of Art: Break Through the Blocks and Win Your Inner Creative Battles.* New York, NY: Black Irish Entertainment LLC.

Pressfield, Steven (1996). *The Legend of Bagger Vance: A Novel of Golf and the Game of Life.* New York, NY: Avon Books, Inc.

Campbell, Joseph (1988). *The Power of Myth.* New York, NY: Random House, Inc.

Laporte, Danielle (2012). *The Fire Starter Sessions: A Soulful + Practical Guide to Creating Success on Your Own Terms.* New York, NY: Harmony Books.

Max, Tucker & Miller Ph. D., Geoffrey (2015). *Mate: Become the Man Women Want. New York, NY:* Little Brown & Company.

Cuelho, Paulo (1993). *The Alchemist.* New York, NY: HarperCollins Publishers Inc.

Burchard, Brendon (2008). *Life's Golden Ticket.* NY: HarperCollins Publishers Inc.
Hawkins, M.D., Ph. D., David R. (1995). *Power VS. Force.* Carlsblad, CA: Hay House, Inc.

Pressfield, Steven (2011). *The Warrior Ethos.* New York, NY: Black Irish Entertainment LLC.

Pressfield, Steven (2012). *Turning Pro.* New York, NY: Black Irish Entertainment LLC.

Pressfield, Steven (1998). *The Gates of Fire.* New York, NY: Bantam Books.

Gray, Ph. D., John (1992). *Men are from Mars women are From Venus.* New York, NY: Quill.

Gray, Ph. D., John (1992). *Mars and Venus on a Date.* New York, NY: Perennial Currents.

Glover, Robert A. (2000) *No More Mr. Nice Guy: A Proven Plan for Getting What You Want in Love, Sex, and Life*. Philadelphia, PA: Running Press.

Ruiz, don Miguel (1997). *The Four Agreements: A Practical Guide to Personal Freedom, A Toltec Wisdom Book*. San Rafael, CA: Amber-Allen.

Chapman, Gary (1992). *The Five Love Languages: The Secret to Love That Lasts*. Chicago IL: Norfield.

Castellano, M.D., Rich (2016). *The Smile Prescription.* New York, NY: Morgan James.

Love, Roger (1999, 2016)). *Set Your Voice Free: How to Get the Singing or Speaking Voice You Want*. New York, NY: Little Brown and Company.

Armstrong, Alison A. (2013). *Celebrating Partnership.* PAX.

Lowndes, Leil (2003). *How to Talk to Anyone: 92 Little Tricks for Big Success in Relationships*. Columbus, OH: McGraw-Hill.

Lowndes, Leil (2001). *Undercover Sex Signals: A Pickup Guide For Guys*. New York, NY: Citadel Press.

Winget, Larry (2013). *Grow a Pair: How to Stop Being a Victim and Take Back Your Life, Your Business, and Your Sanity.* New York: NY: Gotham Books.

Louis, Ron & Copeland, David (1998). *How to Succeed With Women.* Parasmus, NJ. Reward Books.

Dooley, Mike (2010). Manifesting Change, It Couldn't Be Easier. New York, NY: Atria.

Ponder, Catherine (1962). *The Dynamic Laws of Prosperity.* Marina del Rey, CA: DeVoss & Co.

Louis, Ron & Copeland, David (2007) *How to Be The Bad Boy Women Love.* Madison WI, Mastery Technologies.

Eason, Bo. *Personal Story Power.* BoEason.com.

Dyer, Dr. Wayne W. (2004). *The Power of Intention: Learning to Co-create Your World Your Way.* Carlsblad, CA: Hay House.

Lipton Ph.D., Bruce H. (2013). *The Honeymoon Effect: The Science of Creating Heaven on Earth.* Carlsblad, CA: Hay House.

ABOUT THE AUTHOR

Esmée St James first recognized her calling in life as a Confidence Catalyst during her career as a fashion model and professional photographer. Her fascination with the Attractor Factors between the sexes inspired her to launch The Dating Muse™.

As a Dating Strategist for Smart, Serious Singles, her mission is now focused on helping help singles attract their soulmate.

Connect with Esmée via @EsmeeStJames on **Instagram**, **Facebook**, **Twitter**, **Podcast**, and her blog at **TheDatingMuse.com**

While this may seem like, "hot dog, this is the perfect date!" it can have the effect of making a guy feel a little emaciated in the manhood department. It doesn't follow the laws of nature when it comes to courtship. No matter if you are a millennial, genXYZ, yuppie, hippie, baby boomer, octogenarian or a teenager, in my opinion, on the first few dates you should pay the tab.

YOUR PUNCH LIST

Part 1: Your Punch List Summary